"*Force-of-Habit*" (series abstract)

"Only once one knows how something works can it be fully utilized: So it is with us as well."

The knowledge of "**How-We-Work**" is made easily available to everyone in the three books *Force-of-Habit* series. These "**owner's manuals**" inspire not only new views and more useful choices but also massively enhanced living possibilities.

No question one-hundred percent of one's comparative "raw-neurological-data" was provided by sensory accepted "**Bombardment**" from the "**Out-There**". Primarily purposed to enhance survival potential, this "**fodder**" is established in multiple types of "**Soma-Self**" and "**Cognitive- Self**" data-archives.

To everyone's great benefit however, when this "**fodder**" is manipulated and storehoused by multiple "**Cognitive-Self**" mechanisms, its five tier structure also determines the various textures of one's current identity. Fortunately, by understanding how the processes work, one can take control and truly choose outcome.

In order to define **How-We-Work**, *Force-of-Habit*: **Soma-Self** (book-one) begins with sensory origins. It takes the reader on four fun and informative virtual sojourns or journeys through many exciting "**Soma-Self**" mechanisms. It culminates with "**Soma-Habits**", which provide one-half of the "**Force-of-Habit**" dedicated to maximizing survival.

More specifically, *Force-of-Habit*: **Soma-Self** 'journeys' propel the reader from the **Out-There** universe of incessant **Bombardment** or "**Deluge**" to sensory-acceptance. From there one is travelled through multiple data-morphing mechanisms to "**Soma-Actions**": and if the Bombardment is sufficiently-intense, to the "**Cognitive-Alert**" mechanism-array as well, which is designed to engage **Cognitive-Self** for assistance with "**problematic**" issues.

Teaser: Books Two and Three

Force-of-Habit: **Cognitive-Self** (book-two) picks-up where **Soma-Self** leaves off: at the **Cognitive-Alert** assistance-request in-box for **problematic** issues.

> *Force-of-Habit*: **Cognitive-Self** tours the reader through the many and varied mechanisms, constructs and processes, which drive awareness, thought, emotion, ingenuity and one's incredible capacity to **Figure-It-Out** and find **The-Ways**. It explains how emotion plays **THE** vital role in not only data-storage and recall but also the creation of beliefs, personality, behaviour, "**Cognitive-Habits**" and so much more.

Five fascinating "**Cognitive-Pathway**" journeys detail how **Figure-It-Out** is able to expedite "**Solutioning**" for 'sensory-events', which can quickly escalate from nominal to extreme. *Force-of-Habit*: **Cognitive-Self** details how **Figure-It-Out** operates to proactively find **The-Ways** (answers) for both short and extended-term '**questions**' or "**E-Puzzles**" (puzzles) created from either **Bombardment** or from cognitive 'positing' by "**Devise-Mulling's**" intuitive processes.

> Powerfully, **Figure-It-Out** utilizes "**significantly-similar**" 'data-elements' from both (current) data-inbounds and stored data-archives to '**answer**' or **Solution** it's "**Puzzles**".

As **Solution** is being approached, regardless of **Puzzle** origin, both "**Parameter-Processor**" and possibly "**Cognition-Complex**" tailor multiple appropriate-to-puzzle (i.e., appropriate-to-Deluge) outbound-action packet directives called "**Test-It's**". These are configured to spirit cyclical sensory-feedback from the **Out-There** in order to provide incrementing '**answers**' to **Puzzles** (questions) until **Solutioned**.

> Incredibly however, to engage appropriate physical-responders, which in turn 'fodder' one's "**Feedback-Loop**", **Test-It's** are first sent to "**Template-Component**": the transition between the "**In-Here**" cognitive-world and the **Out-There** "**Bombardment-Sphere**" world.

Template-Component first morphs the **Test-It** data-packet to align with internal data-flow and then sends its template-packet to "**Response-Component**" for final outbound configuration. Weather designing or utilizing an existing "**R**esponse-**P**attern", outbound action-packets synchronistically activate physical Soma structures (muscles, etc.), which successively realign one's position within their **Bombardment-Sphere** and therefore drive one away from harm.

Cognitive-Habits, the second half of the **Force-of-Habit** dedicated to maximizing survival, are dedicated to not only significantly enhancing one's **Bombardment-Sphere** 'broader-scope' condition but also mitigating how one's ongoing 'reality' or the "**Movie-of-Your-Life**" is being formulated and presented.

Force-of-Habit: **Implications** (book-three) applies the **How-We-Work** knowledge provided in both *Force-of-Habit:* **Soma-Self** (book-one) and *Force-of-Habit:* **Cognitive-Self** (book-two) to greatly enhance one's practical day-to-day adventures or "**L.I.F.E².**": this author's acronym for "**Living-in-Full-Experience-and-Excitement**".

Specifically, to "**Create-Your-Habits**" and stop letting "**Your-Habits-Create-You**", Book-Three details strategies for successfully not only engaging "**Self-Duo**" to mine "**Habit-Power's**" massive renewable resource but also exploiting **Self-Duo** and "**Cognition-Complex**" to better "**Figure-It-Out**" and find "**The-Ways**".

> The subtitle "**So…How are Your Knobs Doing Anyway**" suggests how chosen **Habit-Power** "Knobs" can be your automatic and continuously vigilant friend, entirely focused on fulfilling your wishes; your dreams: once you fully understand how they function.

Reader Interaction Opportunity:

The *Force-of-Habit* series is intended to inspire ongoing feedback: pros, cons, suggestions, additional detail, enhancements, etc. In that regard DavidHastingsForceofHabit@gmail.com is available for all to contribute what they will: response will be prompt.

> Additionally though, watch for postings on social media sites where more opportunities to provide your thoughts will be offered.

Force-of-Habit: Soma-Self

Book One

Create your habits:

Don't let your habits create you

Produced by:

Living Perspectives Publishing

www.LivingPerspectivesPublishing.com

email: davidhastingsforceofhabit@gmail.com

Force-of-Habit:
Soma-Self

David J. Hastings B.A.

Create your habits:

Don't let your habits create you

For my son Brandon,

Who persistently searches to uncover 'The-Ways':

Inspiring!

Contents

Forward

Everyone is literally pummelled 24/7 by varying quantities and types of external and internal "Bombardment" or "Deluge" events. Although, "external-events" such as noises, smells, tastes, touch and light are instantly identifiable by external sensory apparatus; "internal-events" are not normally discernable until physical structures malfunction resulting in less defined general sensations such as cramps, toothaches, inflammation, joint pain, muscle fatigue and the like.

Regardless of origin, "sensory-accepted" events spawn "data-elements", which are manipulated and morphed by multiple neurophysiological mechanisms. Thus, because data-elements provide one-hundred percent of the "raw-data" and arrays of neurophysiological mechanisms its texture, understanding and appreciating "How-We-Work" must begin with a thorough understanding of both their function and purpose.

In other words, manipulated data-elements not only furnished one-hundred percent of the raw-data determining one's current state-of-perception but also provide the impetus for who one has the potential to become!

4   Force-of-Habit: Soma-Self

Purposed to maximize "survival-potential", two broad groups of "Soma-Self" mechanisms interact: one for "data-acquisition" and one for "data-recall".

Data-acquisition mechanisms initiate with data-element provisioners or sensors; then evolve through multiple uniquely designed mechanisms, which differently retexture data-elements. Ultimately, massaged data-elements not only get "data-archived" in various "data-repositories" but also can trigger "outbound-actions".

Data-recall mechanisms on the other hand provide strategies for data-element retrieval, reconstitution, comparison and possibly, if "sufficiently-intense", integration as "cognitive-constructs": thereby enabling intuition, awareness, assimilation and so much more.

New in concept, connection and interpretation the **Force-of-Habit** trilogy develops comprehensive new outlooks regarding how the Human species not only truly processes bombardment and survives through its seconds, minutes and days but also cognitively embraces possibilities to thrive.

Thus, to accelerate personal growth and make more useful "living-choices", comprehension of the mechanisms driving "How-We-Work" is indispensable: Such is the purpose of the **Force-of-Habit** series.

> **Force-of-Habit** presents new approaches regarding how to think about oneself, one's existence and one's place in our universe.

All are gifted with not one, but two co-operative systems (see "Self-Duo" illustration). The Self-Duo interacts to supply multiple unique processing phases or mechanisms to meet the incredibly difficult challenge of maximizing survival-potential every millisecond of every day.

> Soma-Self, (to the left of the vertical dotted line) as the name implies, manages sensory accepted events originating from body-sensors or "Soma-Sensors" (all sensors except visual – explained later).

"Cognitive-Self" on the other hand, (to the right of the vertical dotted line) accommodates much more complexity. It remarkably handles not only the "Cognitive-Sensor" (visual) "data-stream" but also processes Soma-Self "assistance-requests", which resultantly may require precise inter-lacing with Cognitive-Self and other data-elements.

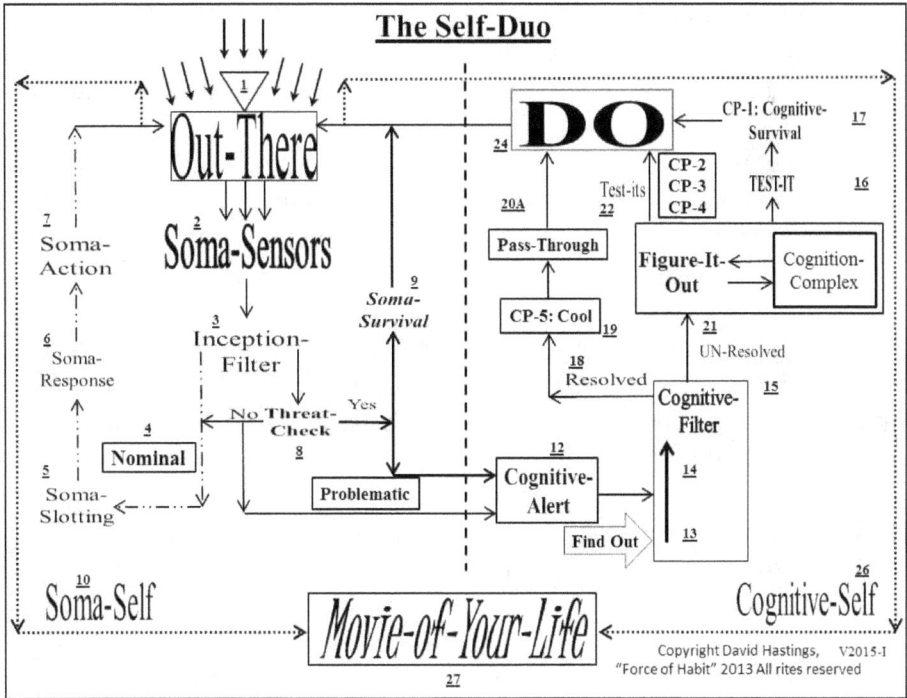

The Self-Duo

Copyright David Hastings,   V2015-I
"Force of Habit" 2013 All rites reserved

Omnibus Framework

The primary mandate for the first two books of the trilogy is to yield a definitive explanation of how we humans roll. Fulfillment will be accomplished by explaining not only mechanism functionalities for each member of the Self-Duo (see illustration below) but also how Soma-Self's (book one) and Cognitive-Self's (book two) numerous operational wonders cooperatively interact to provide all recognition and actualization living potential.

Soma-Self contains two segments: one for presentation and one for in depth detail. The first or story-segment utilizes a narrative format to wonderfully 'travel' the reader through many exciting soma-processes: initiating as a bombardment data-element.

In other words to present comprehensive explanations for How-We-Work, the 'virtual-journey' will take the reader from "Out-There" to "sensory-acceptance" of Bombardment, through conversion and multiple mechanism manipulations, to habitual "Soma-Responses": and beyond.

Although the narrative does not necessarily require detailed background disclosure for general understanding, some may appreciate substantiation of the premises underlying its many newly presented concepts and principles.

> Consequently, when detailed explanations, additional background and/or concept clarity would disrupt narrative flow, the Detailed-Discussion segment (last third or so of the book) will be referenced by insertion of a "DD-identifier".

'Beyond' occurs when Soma-Self cannot 'handle' the bombardment and it requests assistance from Cognitive-Self. Cognitive-Self is thus the focus of book two, which initiates when the Soma-Self's help-me "data-packet" alert is received by "Cognitive-Alert".

Thereby Cognitive-Alert demarcates the pivotal switch-over from Soma-Self to Cognitive-Self mechanisms and processes. Subsequently, data-packet contents initiate a rich array of Cognitive-Self competencies, which determine outcomes from habitual "Cognitive-Responses" to complex behavioral manifestations, cognition, awareness, consciousness, and much, much more.

Book three, **Force-of-Habit: Implications**, subtitled "So-How-are-Your-Knobs-Doing-Anyway", capitalizes on disclosed How-We-Work evidences provided in the first two books. It presents many unique perspectives targeted to positively enhance one's day-to-day adventure or "L.I.F.E². ": this author's acronym for "**Living-in-Full-Experience-and-Excitement**".

Additionally it offers practical applications, whose methodologies concentrate on how to not only "Create-Your-Own-Habits" but also minimize "Your-Habits-Creating-You".

> Expansively, **Force-of-Habit** exposes how one is connected with the Universe; can make more-useful choices; can take control of and get what is truly desired; and much more

As ones living journey inevitably requires "life-choice-actions", intimate understanding of the functioning of driving mechanisms is imperative: i.e., their limitations, diversities and "ultimate-sweet-spots".

Once their true nature is understood, "more-useful" alternatives will be yours for the picking. 'More-useful' choices will definitely enable a much richer and more joyful existence.

Habitual-Nature

Augmenting and integrating the primary How-We-Work mandate, **Force-of-Habit** presents a substantial rethink of the nature and implications of habits. Specifically, "habitual-predisposition" is re-aligned as a tremendous beneficial feature: It will no longer be regarded as a boring inconvenience or limiting handicap.

> **Force-of-Habit** transforms current views of habits into dynamic benefactors enabling one to brightly illuminate and tap into personal, health and financial riches existing all around.

Force-of-Habit explains how habits can be created to happily serve: thereby enabling you to **easily** fulfill desires.

Force-of-Habit trilogy provides irrefutable proof not only detailing the true nature of habits in their entire splendor (there are two types, not just one) but also illuminating effortless strategies to mine their massive, renewable power.

Habits are instantly willing to assist
to get you what you truly want

In the following pages, the exciting ramifications of "Habit-Power" will become brilliantly clear. Once it does, you will be on your way to effortlessly and joyfully living on your chosen terms.

Your enormous dormant potential will be released
once the functioning of both "habit-types" is truly understood

Choicefully created, Habit-Power can be your automatic and continuously vigilant friend, entirely focused on fulfilling your wishes: your dreams.

Force-of-Habit will enable you to propel yourself into developing Habit-Powers, and therefore your extreme untapped potential.

Great news: current patterned habitual-responders can be abandoned, left scampering in the background if you will, and new more useful habits created and adopted!

Force-of-Habit will demonstrate methodologies to easily accomplish creating habits, which will automatically provide huge sustainable benefits. In other words, as paraphrased from book one's sub-title, your possibilities are endless if you:

Create your own <u>new</u> Habits: don't let your <u>old</u> Habits Create You!

Introduction

The graphic below not only illustrates 'Force-of-Habit: Soma-Self' (book-one) journey's but also hints at 'Force-of-Habit: Cognitive-Self' (book-two) adventures.

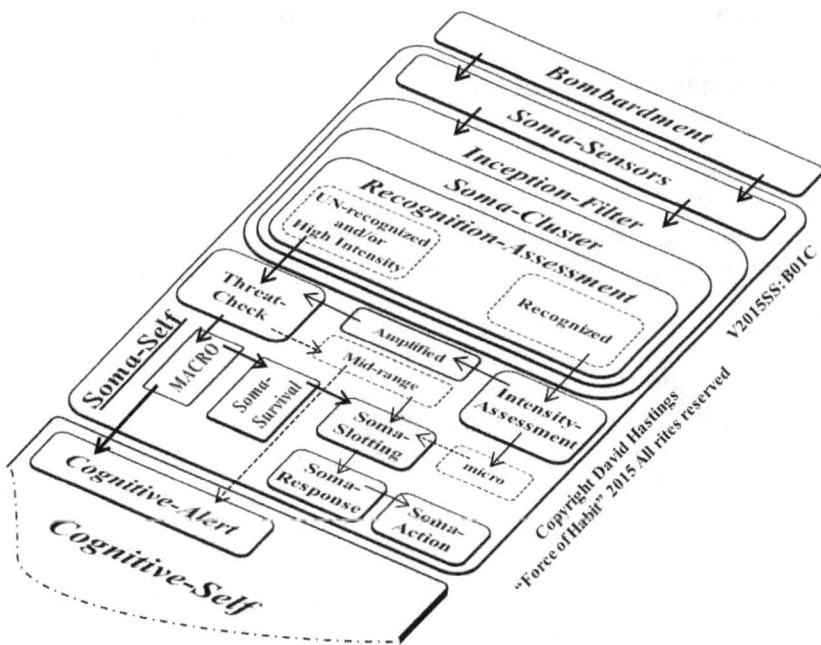

In our current world of technological exploitation, plans to emmulate Human functioning are being devised and evaluated: albeit for servitude by controllable 'intelligent' machines within selfish parameters.

Therefore, as the first two books are the first work to fully disclose what is truly needed to accomplish this mandate an alternate title was considered for this book'.

9 steps to create **Soma-Self** foundations for an android robot, thus enabling the integration of the 23 remaining book two, **Force-of-Habit: Cognitive-Self** protocols for the purpose of actualizing artificial-intelligence and self-awareness!

As a title of this length is frowned upon, I disclose it for two reasons. First, so one might, after digesting the three book series, consider the instigation of consciousness as possible for other species as well: under certain circumstances, as it is for us.

Second, because the principles of 'How-We-Work' in '**Force-of-Habit: Soma-Self**' and '**Force-of-Habit: Cognitive-Self**' can also be employed to indeed create a sentient android robot. Please take this statement as a challenge to make it happen.

Regardless of motivation, truly interactive artificial-intelligence mobile devices require, just as humans do, incorporation of the following **Soma-Self** and **Cognitive-Self** foundational aspects to work effectively and efficiently:

Soma-Self requirements:
- Primary Sensor Platform: Physical Bombardment Impact Receptors
  - Specification for all components used for construction should be of highest quality and allow for near speed-of-light reception, transmission and processing
  - Impact reception
  - Grouped within thousands of variously sized tiny impact or "landing-zones", many tens-of-thousands of sensors, defined by specific acceptance capabilities, should completely cover external-facing surfaces
    - each sensory-accepted event must be 'Tagged' with an immutable location frequency-code or SLID, to uniquely identify it as originating at the event-horizon of a particular sensor-group

- to accommodate for slight variances, frequency-codes must allow for attenuation within a narrow predefined range-of-acceptance at the Soma-Self 'landing-zone'

o Transmission and data-stabilization
  o between event-horizon SLIDs and destination processors, common transmission conduits can be utilized: however they should be supple and allow for movement without signal disruption
  o additionally, an in-line or pre-destination processor platform is required to not only amalgamate the individual "Tag" sensor-signals of a SLID, within short time-snippet 'bands' (3 milliseconds is recommended), into larger common groupings or "Tag-Clusters" but also regulate and thus smooth-out outbound signal groups or 'bands' for...

o Destination processors
  o Ranking 'band' contents ('Tag-Clusters') by greatest quantity of impacts, action-potential or intensity is mandatory to maintain focus on handling highest impact events first; thereby not squandering neural-resources
  o Intensity will be determined by comparing inbound action-potential against range-of-acceptance parameters stored in each SLID compatible destination data-archive
    - When unacceptably high: 'Bracket' and send data-clone to channel-two (see below); otherwise, access frequency specific data-archive to assess event familiarity: i.e., is it new or recurrence
    - dichotomous Recognition-Assessment: YES (recognized) - 'Bracket' and send data-clone to channel-one (see below); Intensity-Assessment: NO (UN-recognized) - 'Bracket' and send data-clone to channel-two; Threat-Check
    - 'handling' requires 'simultaneous' saving, data-archiving or 'Bracketing' by frequency index of sensory-information bits or Tag-Clusters for both channel-one and channel-two

----

- **Channel-One**: Intensity-Assessment for recognized Tag-Clusters
  - o Necessary in case the event has not only occurred before but also carries intensity elevated above acceptable 'nominal' limits
    - ▪ Intensity will also be determined by comparing inbound action-potential against range-of-acceptance parameters stored in each SLID compatible data-archive
    - ▪ 'Elevated-intensity' should be forwarded to processors tuned for 'problematic' assessment: specifically to assess system threat
      - • 'Normal-Intensity' should be sent to 'nominal-channel' for not only 'pattern' creation, which suggests actions for 'Bombardment-Sphere' realignments based on receptor information but also pattern data-archiving
      - • Alert secondary support-system (Cognitive-Self) of changing status so response mechanisms can be initiated and based on imperative for each response location, appropriately sustained and/or tapered-off for smooth operation and transition

- **Channel-Two**: Threat-Check for 'problematic' events
  - o forward to processors tuned for 'problematic' assessment: specifically to assess system "threat-potential" as well:
    - ▪ Intensity-Check to ascertain threat potential from both conduits: Recognition-Assessment high-intensity and Intensity-Assessment 'flags'
    - ▪ Trend-Analysis to assess if event combinations are indicating threat-potential
    - ▪ Issue Cognitive-Alert 'type-one' for survival-critical: 'type-two' if not
    - ▪ Regardless
      - • send upgraded data-packets to 'Soma-Slotting' channel for not only 'pattern' creation, which suggests actions for 'Bombardment-Sphere' realignments based on receptor information but also pattern data-archiving
      - • also for smooth operation and transition, alert secondary support-system (Cognitive-Self) of changing status so response mechanisms can be initiated and based on imperative for each

response location, appropriately sustained and/or tapered-off

----

Cognitive-Self requirements: (Force-of-Habit: Cognitive-Self, book-two teaser)

- Interface System: Cognitive-Alert to collaborator
  - o Translate 'Alerts' into upgraded format

- Secondary Sensor Platform: Visible Spectrum Bombardment receptors
  - o utilize high-tech "Cognitive-Sensors" (vision) to coordinate and augment Soma-Sensory data-flow
  - o where applicable to provision broader event perspective, combine Soma-Sensor and Cognitive-Sensor data into a more representative Cross-Sensory data-pool
    - ▪ determine intensity as 'NORM' or 'PRIORITY'
  - o If NORM 'Tepid' or PRIORITY 'Warm' or 'Hot', engage "Figure-It-Out" Cognitive-Pathways
  - o Otherwise deploy on 'Cool' Cognitive-Filter pathway

- Engage Figure-It-Out
  - o Bring resources on-line as applicable: such as, Equivalency, Resolution, Initialization and Parameter processors to find 'The-Ways'
  - o Update 'Data-Matrix' data-archives
  - o Create 'Puzzles' and evaluate against data-archives utilizing Cognition-Complex's Delving-Trio and Devise-Mulling
  - o Create Test-It outbounds to prompt 'Out-There' feedback

- Engage 'Template-Component' to create patterns alerting Soma-Self of required 'Out-There' positional 'DO' adjustments or outbound actions

- Continually produce and present, without pause or break, the 'Movie-of-Your-Life' from sensory-and-archive data-streams

Sound familiar…?

Force-of-Habit: Soma-Self' Prelude

Soma-Sensor varieties are many. They provide uniquely delineated zones of contact purposed to 'inform' what is going on 'Out-There'. As 'Out-There' is considered to be all pre-sensory events, internal-sensors are also included.

Our biology is laced with tiny Bombardment impact collectors or 'event-horizons' called SLIDs or Soma-Location-IDs: from which the abbreviated name is contrived. Each SLID receptor-neuron array is not only an ever diligent recipient of raw 'mechanical' Deluge impact-data when not in 'refresh-state' but also discretely identifiable by a unique frequency, which remains immutable throughout processing, data-archiving and recall.

Additionally, although common transmission conduits are utilized by all SLIDs (Soma-Location-IDs) to transfer sensory-receptor information to brain-mass, each ends at its own dedicated neuron-array, which only accepts its specific SLID frequency marker.

> More specifically Neuro-physiological sensory-receptor design provides SLIDs with their own exacting bent on a sensory occurrence.

In other words, SLIDs possesses their own specific and immutable frequency-ranged recognition signatures, which forever identify the acceptance location and content. 'Marking' thereby ensures identification of both sensory-type and the specific sensory impact point, which is essential for both 'recognition' and recall.

> This strategy also ensures a sound is not confused with touch, smell or taste: neither during data-archiving nor data-recall.

Additionally critical to measure is 'event-intensity'. It is highly variable due to not only the types and quantity of SLID locations involved as a consequence of highly variable Bombardment but also the quantity of accepted events as a factor of short-to-longer Deluge duration, neuron firing patterns, neuron activity-duration and neuron recovery time.

> Even so, event-intensity is not determined at time-of-impact but further up the processing chain at Recognition-Assessment. Here, the quantity of neurons fired at each SLID within a 3 millisecond "time-snippet" or "data-band" are evaluated to determine 'intensity'

and therefore next disposition: to either 'nominal' or 'problematic' conduit.

After "sensory-acceptance", the Soma-Self cycle initiates with "Inception-Filter", which "Filters-and-Slots" all accepted "sensory-data".

Subsequently, "Recognition-Assessment" directs the "data-stream" into one or the other of two channels: either to 'UN-recognized', which includes high-intensity or 'recognized', which does not.

Whereas 'UN-recognized' and/or high-intensity are immediately fired to "Threat-Check" as 'problematic', the 'recognized' data-stream is shunted to "Intensity-Assessment" for additional evaluation.

If its verdict is 'nominal-intensity', Tag-Clusters are shuttled to "Soma-Slotting": those which are not 'nominal-intensity' are also sent to Threat-Check for 'problematic' analysis.

> Additionally, as assessments are finalized in "Soma-Action", the Endocrine-System is additionally apprised. As a supporting "Integration-System", it is designed to ensure response mechanisms gracefully transition through a three stage "action-cycle": thereby providing smooth operation and movement.

The Endocrine-System utilizes notifications to appropriately prepare "action-sites" for activation from rest or 'nominal' state. 'Appropriate' is based on the "ranked-imperative" about to be neuro-transmitted to each response location from Soma-Action.

Secondly, it provides variable impetus to sustain action-site activity and/or "action-alertness" after neurological signals have ceased. Thirdly, the Endocrine-System allows for a tapering-off period so action-sites can 'gracefully' return to 'normal' state and refresh.

Finally, Soma-Self tethers to "Cognitive-Self" by creating two distinct Cognitive-Alert "data-package" outbounds: both shaped differently by Threat-Check. Notwithstanding the content and imperative variances between the two data-packages, both are designed to initiate Cognitive-Self assistance to 'Figure-It-Out'.

By the issuance of Cognitive-Alerts, Soma-Self provides
the first-half of the

Force-of-Habit

which champions species sustainability.

Cognitive-Alerts provide a valuable clue to purposefully and massively enhancing ones "living-situation" by underlining THE requisite to engage Cognitive-Self at will!

As long as an event is either new or of higher intensity, exciting if you will, 'recognized and low-intensity' Soma-Habitual responses will be augmnented by mid-range Threat-Check processors, which will produce Cognitive-Alerts.

> This outbound is critical because Cognitive-Alert is the only opportunity to initiate Cognitive-Self; and therefore the opportunity for awareness and conscious choice!

Book-two's mandate is to comprehensively delve into Cognitive-Self to expose "How-We-Work" as a cognitive species: because once Cognitive-Selfs many incredible capabilities are grasped, your massive potential will be unleashed.

Resultantly, once one knows 'how-they-work', will not only 'day-to-day' situations be clearly understood from a "more-useful" perspective but also "choiceful-living" be significantly energized.

Beginnings

The weekend finally arrives...Saturday morning...hurrah! Excited to meet up with your golfing buddies, get to the course and get playing you quickly pack your golf clubs into the trunk. Into the car, out the driveway and down the road you go. As you are executing a perfect left turn you chuckle to yourself because left is the turn you take each weekday to get to work: the golf course, is right.

When similar situations occur most think something like, "habit I guess".

So what went on when the weekday left turn was taken, instead of the weekend right turn?

It turns out to energize this simple event two incredible multi-faceted systems engaged: Soma-Self (SS) and Cognitive-Self (CS). Incredibly, collaborative deployment of their component mechanisms align and respectively define everyone's Biological/Physiological and Psychological/Cognitive interaction with...well everything.

Awareness something exists is insufficient to realize its potential: knowing how 'the something' truly works however creates vast possibilities.

'The Self's' Overview

Notably, in this author's opinion, Soma-Self and Cognitive-Self are the greatest symbiotic relationship of all time: giving and receiving freely without conflict. Their nature is our nature; if we choose to understand.

We can live naturally and in balance: the model is US

Soma-Self has a primary directive - a single purpose: survival. To provide optimal survival conditions Soma-Self utilizes its "data-archive" to determine the dichotomous status of each inbound "data-element", either recognized or UN-recognized, to select next-steps.

For recognized "sensory-events" Soma-Self drives data-elements toward Habitual auto-responses, which by the very nature of offering no cognitive interface are not only very fast but also transparent to (do not alert) Cognitive-Self.

However, when a data-event is UN-recognized and/or high intensity, Soma-Self not only continues to stock its data-archive by "Filtering-and-Slotting" the UN-recognized "sensory-data" but also requests assistance from its Cognitive-Self collaborator by sending notification to Cognitive-Alert.

> The Cognitive-Alert "outbound-link" (outbound from Soma-Self's perspective) is of critical importance because it alone enables cognitive process by providing the only "up-link" interface between Soma-Self and Cognitive-Self

Cognitive-Self is charged dually to not only "Figure-It-Out" but also craft feedback-requests, which are destined to be actioned by Soma-Self sensors. Cognitive-Self accomplishes fulfillment of Soma-Self's assistance requests by deploying several Modules and many Components, which actualize 'real' world interaction by deploying a huge arsenal of sophisticated methodologies: discussed in Force-of-Habit book two: Cognitive-Self.

Unlike Soma-Self, which operates in milliseconds, the much slower Cognitive-Self unfolds its processes in cognitively manageable second time slices. Additionally compounding this difference, Cognitive-Self data-repositories are vastly larger and more complex than Soma-Self's, whose neural-real-estate is built for speed, not complexity.

Resultantly, for Cognitive-Self to "keep-up" it deploys continually hone-able "Cognitive-Habits", which are delivered as assumptions. Once "experience-archives" reach sufficient proportion (typically in late puberty) they become Cognitive-Self's 'front-line' immediate "habitual-responders".

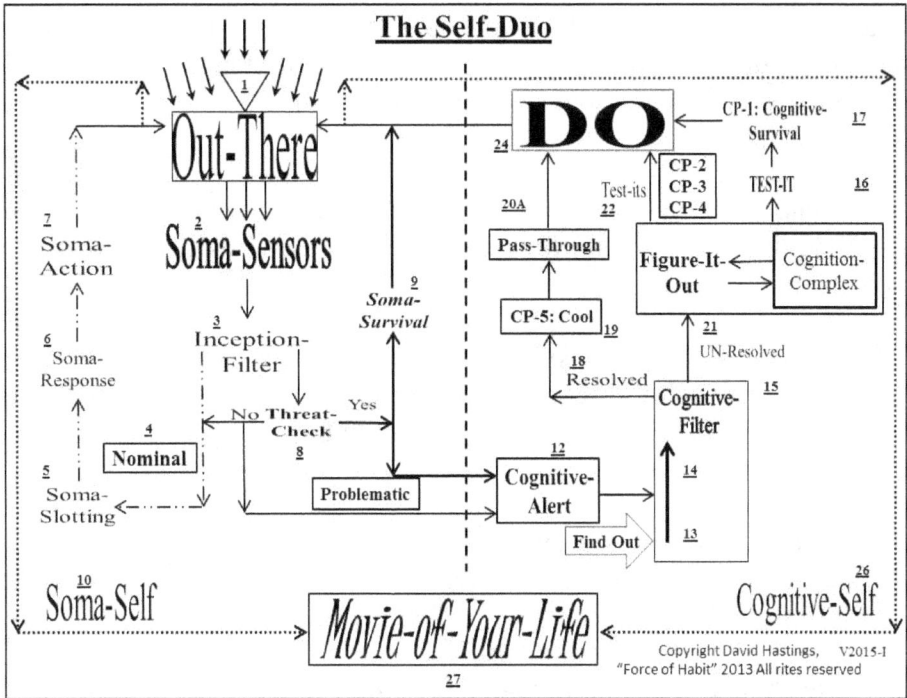

The Self-Duo

So like Soma-Self, Cognitive-Self is also driven or predisposed by genetics to create habits to ensure survival. The difference is 'survival' for Cognitive-Self is expanded to encompass the creation of superior living conditions: Thereby, Cognitive-Habits exhibit much broader purview.

Even more complexly, Cognitive-Self has a stringent mandate, which is substantially different, from Soma-Self's survival focus. It must seamlessly present its personalized version of reality I call the "Movie-of-Your-Life".

Cognitive-Self must provide and/or devise the Movie-of-Your-Life, from whatever combinations of sources are accessible: current sensory-data, experiences from "data-repositories", assumptions and/or imagination from "Cognition-Complex". Its presentation must be unbroken, without 'static' interference, or our universe interaction would be jerky, not smooth and continuous. In other words, the mandate is to load all the "movie-of-your-life-frames" with content: no exceptions and no blanks.

The "Self-Duo" illustration (additionally reproduced above) provides a condensed guideline for tracking our upcoming journey through Soma-Self (to the left of the vertical dotted line) and on into Cognitive-Self (to its right).

As each step is numbered, think of this graphic as a high-level outline of discussion progression for Books one and two. To enhance clarity as we progress, this initial illustration will be augmented by other depictions and offerings.

Once Soma-Self and Cognitive-Self mechanisms and processes are understood, tapping into and fully utilizing their myriads of facilities with which all are gifted, will be possible.

> The most exciting upside: when one knows 'how-one-truly-works' "more-useful" choices will become evident and therefore will avail dramatically enhanced 'living' opportunities.
>
> ---
>
> However, before we embark on our journey by opening the first door to uncover the miracle of us, a few stepping-stones require exposure. First, how does all we are get started?

To initiate their magic, both 'Self's' employ various front-line arrays of specialized and unique event-horizon information gathering receptors or sensors: specifically, "Soma-Sensors" and "Cognitive-Sensors". Genetically moulded, sensors are fabricated to have 'first-go' at accepting or rejecting (sensory) "Bombardment" or "Deluge".

> Biologically speaking Soma-Self provides all sensory-devices except sight (visual-reception), which is actually a Cognitive-Self multiple-sensory apparatus (explanations further along)

All creatures unquestionably rely on "sensory-arsenals", which provide dozens of 'collectors' to provide front-line 'news'. Sensory-mechanisms initiate not only an event-chain, which enables precise navigation through the tumultuous chaos of external and internal sensory bombardment but also the "data-stream", whose "data-elements" form the basis for all one is and will become.

Bombardment or Deluge

No doubt we exist in a cacophony of activity where representatives of every force in the universe, at some point, either come to impact (bombard) our outer "receptor-shell" or flow right through us (see 'Deluge' illustration below). For a 'normal-day' without 'unusual' occurrences, Deluge or impacting "bombardment-events" are estimated in the neighborhood of about two hundred thousand per second. Therefore, discussing "sensor-speed" is going to be a necessity.

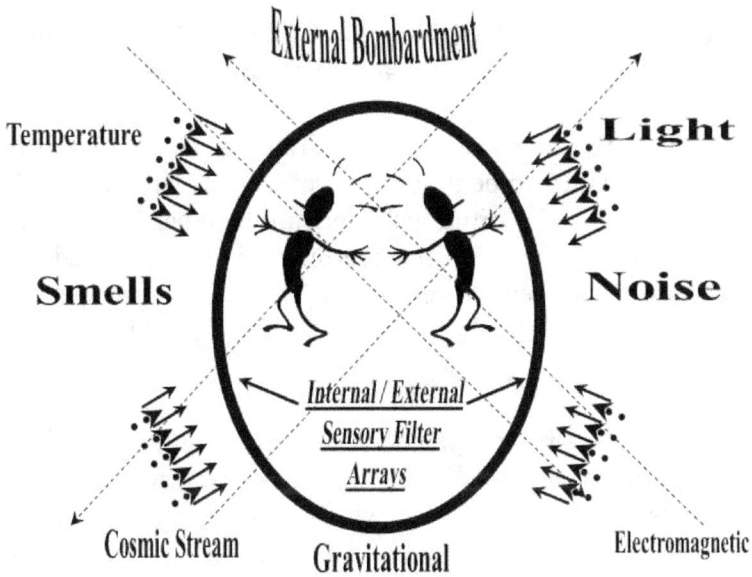

Deluge

Of course, depending on activity "sensory-impact" quantities fluctuate greatly: i.e., much fewer while peacefully sleeping; much more while jumping from a perfectly good airplane. Generally then, 'the-count' is dependent on not only how finely potential impact bits are "sensory-sliced" but also the current peace or turmoil of influencing environments.

Both external and internal origins are responsible for delivering Bombardment to sensory "event-horizons". Externally, Deluge is comprised of not only "sensor-recognizable" incidents (more on what this means below) like light and noise but also transparent or "sensor-imperceptible" events: such as the thousands of created radio frequencies; gravity; a whole vast array of cosmos generated electromagnetic frequencies; and so on.

Significant bombardments are also produced by internal events: also either recognized or not. For instance, the "sensor-initializing" conditions, which result in sensation of an upset stomach or fatigued muscle group are recognized: whereas transparent is a decline in blood pH due to a build-up of carbon dioxide, which bombards several "internal-sensors" (in this case chemoreceptors), thereby signaling it's time to take a breath.

> Taken as a whole, the commotion is massive. It is incredible survival is even possible in such conditions.

So the big question is, "What has kept us safe by 'handling' these many incredibly variant external and internal bombardment-events?"

Sensory-receptor characteristics and capabilities at the receiving boundary (event-horizon) of bombardment activity definitively provide the 'starting-line' part of the answer. Fortuitously, not all bombardment is accepted: determination is up to the "sensory-neuron" being bombarded. "Sensory-filtering" is in place for several reasons, which will be provided as Soma-Self's mysteries are unravelled (items 1 through 11 on "Self-Duo" illustration).

> Soma-Self sensory-acceptance is just the beginning of the journey. Onward from there, the excursion is replete with fascinating mechanisms and processes, which "Filter-and-Slot" Soma-Self's data-stream: then catapults onward into Cognitive-Self...if conditions are 'right' (items 12 through 24 on 'Self-Duo' illustration)!

What are Habits?

Classically, the definition of 'a habit' goes something like this: a habit is any automated behavior (auto-response) and/or function occurring with little or no awareness or (necessary) cognitive interception.

Contained within this definition, which at first seems simple and self-evident, are significant, perhaps unclear, fundamental concepts, which raise pertinent questions requiring clarification, such as: What is 'a' habit; what is auto-response; how can habits occur with little or no awareness; what is cognitive interception; how are habit and cognitive aspects related or interrelated?

Answers to these questions and many more will be detailed below but first some fundamentals.

Our current concept of 'a habit' as a stand-alone process is totally incorrect from any viewpoint: Neuro-physiologically; genetically; psychologically; etc. It is an old and outdated mono-dimensional and limiting concept. Initiators attempted in an inaccurate global way to explain human behaviour without really committing to anything substantial.

Although the classical "habit" definition is not functional, there are obviously biological (Soma-Self) auto-responses (Soma-Habits). These events seem to occur spontaneously (from our Cognitive-Self view), without any detailed vigilant awareness: biological auto-response events such as, breathing, heartbeat, smoking, etc. Potential to interface and directly change many of these is scarce.

Also evident are cognitive auto-responses (Cognitive-Habits). Most (upwards of 80%) of these events also seem to occur spontaneously. The difference being one can choose to become aware of most of them and perform adjustments: i.e., a few of these potentially aware events are walking, running, speaking, thinking, etc.

Globally speaking, upwards of 90% of our daily outcomes are habitually driven by either Soma-Habits or Cognitive-Habits: about 65% Soma-Habits and 25% Cognitive-Habits. Additional habits include answering, self-talk, eating, work routines, sports, vast numbers of biological processes, and the list goes on.

Some of these Cognitive-Habits may have been purposefully created but now mostly run on auto-pilot such as: practised athletic endeavors; musician prowess; picking up a fork; writing; the wrong turn above; etc.

In all significant respects we are therefore, without doubt, a Habitual Species: mostly driven throughout our existence not by conscious choice but by intrinsic, pervasive auto-responders, which are our deepest nature. 'Habits', with their ability to rapidly respond us to safety, have always been and will continue to be the pervasive 'Force' behind our survival: in other words, one survives because **Force-of-Habit** is inescapable.

Force-Of-Habit Power

Incredibly, if one combined "Soma-Habit" and Cognitive-Habit output, this duo, let's call them "Habit-Duo", would account for 'mechanically' running most (upwards of 95%) of one's 'normal' day. Resultantly, they represent not only THE focal survival agent control devices but also with a different spin, THE provisioner of our greatest advantage.

Why would this be so one might ask? After all if 95% of our day is controlled by habitual-responses, whether from Soma-Self and/or Cognitive-Self, how can Habit-Duo also be "THE provisioner of our greatest advantage"?

Let me suggest the following. You are in possession of two very powerful mechanisms: Soma-Self and Cognitive-Self. Up to this juncture most have disregarded and/or been minimally aware of their power: i.e., how they harness resources and processes to get-the-job-done.

The exception, although most again do not think of it in these terms, which everyone relies on to work is 'practice. One knows if you practice (repetition) over and over your skills will improve based on your interest in acquiring the skill of course.

> To be clear this is you creating Soma-Habits and Cognitive-Habits for the purpose of getting you what you want. Big exclamation and Key: get you what you truly want; not what you think you might want. (Much more is provided on this topic as we progress.)

Even though Habit-Duo is our most staunch ally and champions most of our daily responses, most consider it inconsequential. We much prefer to think of ourselves as a cognitive species fully in control of all our actions. We were never informed that Habit-Duo is our strongest supporter and will seamlessly fulfill all our hopes and dreams.

Think of Habit-Duo as your personal "Dream Fulfillment Team"

Make no mistake; Habit-Duo is a huge genetic gift provided to everyone without exception.

It will automatically and effortlessly (that's its inherent design) deliver all your dreams and desires once you fully understand how Soma-Self and Cognitive-Self work individually and in harmony. Once understood, one can even turn "Habit-Duo-Power" up to high - or at least up a few notches

What are Mechanisms?

Definition-wise a mechanism is a tangible thing or a routinized system or systems created or adapted to perform a particular task or sequences of similar tasks. To perform a mechanism utilizes a predefined series of procedures or techniques as delineated by a plan.

More clearly, interpret Force-of-Habit mechanisms as specific purpose processing stations, which may or may not utilize virtual "data-resources" for "data-manipulations" and/or existing "data-archives" as reference sites.

Generally, each mechanism accepts a previous mechanisms morphed data-stream, manipulates or filters contents according to mechanism requirements and then sends the morphed "data-packet" on (Slots it) to a follow-on mechanism.

Soma-Self purview encompasses arrays of supporting mechanisms and processes designed to maximize survival-potential for the physical body (soma), where sensory information originated with body or "Soma-Sensors". Stated differently, Soma-Self deals with all soma-sensor initiated processes. These do not directly impact 'higher' brain function but instead utilize dedicated less dynamic Soma-Self brain mass.

Both Soma-Habit and most Cognitive-Habits have their roots or initialize as sensory input. There is a particular immutable event processing flow: Soma-Self to Cognitive-Self, then back to Soma-Self. They participate in an ever changing loose to dense entanglement of connected activity presenting various textures, types and intensities, which have been forged by millions of years of survival diligence.

Force-of-Habit has therefore redefined "habit" to mean all Soma-Habit's and all Cognitive-Habit's, which interactively present to contribute their parts to how we experience the "Movie-of-Your-Life"

What are Sensory-Systems?

Everything we are and everything we have potential to become is wholly dependent on the ability of each persons "sensory-system" to accept information, which is pertinent for it and reject what is not. They are the border-guards or the "touch-point" between the "Out-There" (see 'Self-Duo' illustration above) and all "data-elements" (data-package granular contents) archived by the diverse mechanisms of Soma-Self and Cognitive-Self, which makes one unique.

Believing sensory-systems are understood, some at this juncture may be tempted to skip this section. However, it is imperative to realize the educational system critically misinformed regarding most of their aspects: such as, how critical sensory-systems are to living; what senses do; how many there are (way more than five); and how they work.

Resultantly, reading on will provide definite benefits. Without question previous information promoted huge misunderstanding and therefore disservice to an amazing array of front-line structures. It is more-useful to think of these diverse collectors as gifts, structured to not only 'handle' all reception but also provide the data-streams containing information on "what is going on Out-There". They are after all the initiators of sentience (awareness or consciousness).

A 'normal-day' for a sensor-array is to be pounded on 24/7: a tough, very busy situation in any evaluation. How this is accomplished is an amazing story, essential to be told and understood: for 'Force-of-Habit' purposes for sure.

> Identifying sensory-array shared operational parameters is critical to understand How-We-Work from sensory-acceptance to habitual-responses through proactive cognitive manipulations, which initiate auto-responses and 'chosen' behavioural interactions with 'Out-There'.

In other words, sensory-system common functionalities such as data-stream creation and characteristics must first be disclosed. Only then can the potential to enable sentience from data-element (an accepted and transformed elemental piece of a data-stream) manipulations and intermixing be fully understood and appreciated.

Recall from above, instead of including a large piece of important "break-out" information or proofing within the flow of a section, book one is comprised of two distinct segments: the segment being read now and a "Detailed-Discussion" (DD) segment, housed in the last third or so of this book. Deploying this strategy accommodates not only minimal interruption to the 'flow' as we proceed but also quick review access by using the provided cross-reference identifier.

The first set of 'break-out' information details "The-Senses". This reference section is presented under the "DD-001" identifier in the Detailed-Discussion (DD) Segment. I recommend reading the indicated section now and harvesting what is comfortable for you. Please bookmark and reread excerpts as appropriate to clarify future discussions.

Notably then from 'DD-001' discussions, many mechanisms comprise a Sensory-System. Like a great documentary, lots of co-ordinated effort is occurring behind the scenes to ensure correct handling. In humanities case, survival is at stake; and survival depends on everything working in harmony with everything else.

If one had to cognitively process or think what to do with and then accurately manage each of the speeding thousands of streaming individual events arriving at one soma-sensory event-horizon each millisecond, there would be a massive cognitive system failure. Our Cognitive-Self is, quite simply, not designed for this quantity of raw-data inundation: It is way, WAY too slow in relation to its more complex mandates!

The good news, a group of Soma-Self mechanisms is correctly designed for the task. It works many times faster than its "Cognitive-Assistant" because it is built for speed; not complexity (explanation to come). When coupled with its supporting receivers and interlaced communication networks, Soma-Self can easily handle or "Filter-and-Slot" this torrent. As a reminder, when exceptions occur, Soma-Self engages Cognitive-Self by forwarding a data-packet to Cognitive-Alert.

Soma-Self sensory-acceptance is just the beginning of a journey, replete with fascinating mechanisms and processes: through Soma-Self and onward into Cognitive-Self…if conditions are 'right'!

Master Blueprint: Ranges

Let's face it…there is one irrefutable commonality…one aspect identical for everyone and everything…we don't get to vote on it…agreement is a default: We all live in the same universe.

At first this might seem a little trite, but let me explain. We do not get to make any rules. If not provided for by the Physical Laws of the Universe we are simply out of luck. Most, when thinking of the universe, visualize a vast realm existing "out there": That belief is a misperception.

> Not surprisingly, the universe does not stop at our skin but encompasses every aspect of functionality within as well as around us. Everything that rules the universe then, rules us as well.

A major specification of this universe, important for all discussions to come, is "ranges": although gradient extents vary, everything has a lowest value to a highest value. Looked at with this perspective our human selves are a culmination of a huge number of very different systems expressing their own unique "ranges-of-operability".

Each system is reliant on its design range: within which it works and outside of which it doesn't. For instance, galaxies have size ranges; stars have life spans, as do we; there is a visible light range; atoms, molecules and compounds are defined by frequency ranges; there are sensation ranges; recipes provide ingredients with specified quantities (fixed ranges); and so on.

Ranges in Force-of-Habit are also termed "Gradient-of-Acceptability". These "GOA's" encompass energy ranges, corporeal function ranges, non-corporeal reality ranges and non-tangible ranges, like brightness and feelings.

Additionally, because our "Universe-Home" has provided all the materials and permissible combinations, no-one has ever discovered anything from scratch. In a very real sense one only uncovers what has always been there.

This is fantastic news!

This open-ended design, allowing broad-range experience, emancipates one's potential: i.e., no intrinsic narrow-band limiter is at play.

The true limiter, as will soon be appreciated, is an extremely resilient worst habit: "The-Way-We-Think". Force of Habit is very clear on how this self-imposed limiter can be choice-fully and positively recreated (much more on that later in book three).

Universe Container

Our 'universe container' seemingly provides two components: energy and material. Notably, material is comprised from the former: so in one regard then, only one building block.

Critical to understand because both corporeal and non-corporeal (living and inanimate) participants are formed from universe material and must abide by its energy rules. Thus these 'two' building-blocks bind everything and everyone together.

"What does universe talk have to do with Force of Habit"?

The answer, as you will soon see, is 'everything'. Universal material and energy provision creates our fundamental components: both are fundamentally the same but seem different depending on the level of granularity being assessed.

If asked, are you built from energy convergence or matter, the answer is both. Component parts (foundational origins) not only define the very essence of the universe but also our physical existence and current deployment as humans.

There is a common fundamental feature responsible for the success of the universe and for our survival: most (perhaps all) material and energy combinations work in absolute, predictable and repeatable ways. This is also absolutely true within our biological machine (body) as well.

Depending on perspective, the universe parts are simultaneously in states of stability and of flux. All rely on the suns energy to be continually available: stability.

Simultaneously though, one exists because exploding stars created all the more complex elemental building-blocks (discrete atomic amalgams) of which one is formed.

Amazingly, it is those stable matter/energy interactions, which also champion our physical and cognitive functioning.

Neural Pathways Project: Soma-Self

Sojourn: SS-One & SS-Two

Team-1 Chronicles

To say 'journeys' necessitated extraordinary preparation
would be a substantial understatement

Cytoons dream of 'traveling' neural-pathways suddenly sparked into a real possibility. While editing a cutting edge paper for a physicist friend on seemingly unrelated Black-Hole research, it became evident to her the breakthrough research being documented could significantly catapult her project forward. Before that though, she was ready to throw in the towel.

In a conversation with me a couple of years back, I am 'Team-1' leader Retic and this journey's commentator by the way, Cytoon confided she was actually about to put five years of research to uncover "How-We-Work" from sensory-input through to behavioral and cognitive manifestations, on the back-burner.

Even though still passionate she confided, to conclusively comprehend the flow-of-events from sensory origins, through neural-pathways and to final disposition within the brains neural-arrays, blockades to accurate data-gathering seemed insurmountable.

> Her research was ineffective Cytoon stated mostly due to "antiquated and insufficient technical innovation", which precluded gathering adequate and reliable "real-data".

Therefore, she continued project termination seemed her only prudent course of action. Cytoon, now Team-1's Neuro-physiologist, elaborated by stating after hundreds of attempts she was unable to satisfactorily acquire 'real-data' either from millisecond bombardment events occurring at neuron event-horizons or by tracking transformed "data-elements" within a concurrently populated "data-stream". Obvious to me Cytoons project was no easy mission.

Cytoon divulged after trying many workarounds, it became obvious the only way to get precise and significant information would be to actually travel-along with the data-stream, encounter mechanisms, then observe and record data-element transmogrifications. Thus, as this requisite seemed impossible research termination was prudent she stated.

> Little did Cytoon realize her multitudes of attempts had set the stage for a most amazing series of "Neural-Pathways" journeys, which would truly redefine "How-We-Work".

Fortunately, Cytoons "Neural-Pathways" project enthusiasm had remained strong. If it hadn't, her meeting with Black-Hole researchers, which provided a critical key, may never have occurred.

For it was in her first discussion they confirmed Black-Hole studies uncovered not only several unknown and fascinating universe features but also one, which could actually enable her to accomplish a "miniaturization-journey": its tenet was termed "Size-Irrelevance".

What escalated Cytoons excitement to peak however was when they told her miniaturization methodologies, although incredibly difficult to decipher, had just been ratified: and therefore her miniaturization-requirement was absolutely achievable…theoretically.

> Cytoon stated she was more than excited about the rebooted project as it would "provide the means to finally define and explain the myriads of individual mechanisms, which form the collaborative set of biological, physiological and neurological tools rousing the bio-electrical machine called Homo Sapiens into sentience".

Consequently, now notions once considered more a fantasy than likely were proven possible, the following two years engrossed Cytoon and her teams who worked diligently to satisfy their ever growing wish list. As research progressed, obvious was extreme technological innovations would additionally be required to overcome an ever growing list of ponderous compounding difficulties.

I discovered complexly was greater than originally estimated because the equipment and techniques provided by the black-hole researchers required scaling-up: extensively.

As it turned out, their teams had only 'shrunk' an orange to molecular size: and although size re-normalized it, the 'orange' was never checked to validate reconstitution was free of anomalies. Therefore, what Cytoon was attempting, to shrink then perfectly reconstitute a fully equipped 'vehicle' of some sort was massively more demanding.

For instance Cytoon stated, if the 'vehicle' was going to have any chance of being 'accepted' by the targeted sensory-neurons, its 'footprint' must exactingly mimic three conditions, which must closely align within narrow parameters: vibrational frequency; bombardment activation intensity; and physical configuration or molecular vibration.

Additionally Cytoon continued, determining the 'pre-shrunk' optimal 'vehicle' size and shape was dependent on not only developing and fabricating appropriate materials for the 'shell' but also the spatial and weight bearing requirements of installed data-gathering equipment.

She added, the 'shell' material for the mimicking 'vehicle' was especially difficult to determine. The shell-compound had to not only allow precise mimicking of the original vibrational attributes of the molecule chosen to be the Bombardment event but also facilitate multiple transmutations or re-mimics during its 'journey' as an accepted data-element.

As well Cytoon elaborated, other concerns abounded: such as, how to maintain control while at reduced size; how to recover the 'vehicle'; how to 'normalize' its size once retrieved; how to gather sufficient data; how to frame and present the gathered data; and the list went on she said.

> In less than a year and a half Cytoon accomplished the seemingly impossible! She and her teams perfected techniques to not only 'shrink' a specifically configured "Emulation-Vehicle" or "EV" to molecular size but also modulate the EV shell to precisely impersonate the real thing.

As incredible as EVs are, science-teams went leaps further by designing, testing and implementing several other unique and incredible journey enhancing key technologies as well. Foremost, a multifaceted "Artificial-Intelligence-Matrix" ("AIM" for short) was architected to perform not only guidance-system and system-controller functions but also several other needed functions: such as data-gathering, compression recording, data-decoding, data-interpretation, visual-rendering and many other tasks.

> Cytoon confided a huge desire: to be able to, even if only partially, interpret and visually render amassed data on some sort of interactive display apparatus.

Science-teams Cytoon excitedly stated surprised and exceeded all expectations by not only creating "DiHol", a "Three-Dimensional-Holographic-Display" device and interfacing it to AIM but also developing 'anticipatory-programs', which enabled the on-board artificial-intelligence-matrix (AIM) flexibility to perform both autonomous dynamic interpretation and fluid format presentation.

The DiHol viewing platform was no less incredible Cytoon said. Designed to fully maximize DiHol's three dimensional holographic display capabilities, an observer or "virtual-traveler" as they came to be called would tether themselves into a gyroscopic chair.

Located at the center of DiHol's spherical holographic display the virtual-traveler had two options: Either be automatically positioned by AIM toward new projected data renderings or choose manual-mode, pause the 'virtual-replay' and leisurely move the "gyro-chair" to view displays.

> Regardless, it will be interesting to see AIM renderings with actual journey data she said.

Now necessary technology was available, Cytoon knew she was on the brink of not only realizing her dream but expanding it to even broader-scope. Resultantly, I have observed multitudes of meetings with all teams during the previous six months to define and redefine Journey-One parameters and goals. I am excited to share their determinations, knowing Team-1 will soon be off 'traveling'.

Journey-One Parameters and Goals

Although probably already evident from the above commentary, to openly share this momentous Journey-One experience was unanimously agreed. By so doing all hoped the resulting anthology would enable future researchers and interested parties to not only enjoy the journeys 'virtual-experience' but also come to truly understand "How-We-Work".

Optimistically, the Journey-One narrative will become a primary resource for comprehending Soma-Self functionality from pre-sensory origins through "Soma-Response" (items 1-9 on the Self-Duo illustration located in the Detailed-Discussion segment at DD-002).

Several resources will contribute to the anthologies content and format. The 'trip-adventure' portion will present the 'actual' journey details as an 'adventure-narrative' of sorts.

> 'Actual' specifics of necessity will be derived from a few sources: 'virtual-traveler' recorded observations as a participant interacts with presented "AIM" (Artificial-Intelligence-Matrix) renderings on "DiHol" (Three-Dimensional-Holographic-Display); pertinent scientific addendums; plus general journey impressions gleaned from the vantage point of actually flowing along with the data-stream in 'real-time'.

In support of the story-line, the ancillary objective is to describe what was necessary to actualize this journey. Thus, the narrative will begin by providing various backgrounds of how Journey-One came to be. For additional clarity, selected journey organizational rationale will also be inserted here-and-there when applicable.

> Globally then, Journey-One is intended to explore and report on a 'sensory-event' to elucidate the causality and define the granularity of what is truly at work within our neuro-physiological containers.

Narrative will begin from "Out-There" and progress to a single Bombardment impact on a selected sensory-receptor array. After clarifying sensory-acceptance, tracking will continue through multiple sensory inspired mechanisms and processes to illuminate characteristics of their neurophysiological inner-world.

The ultimate goal of the omnibus is to explain sensory-inspired manifestations such as habitual actions, memory, recall, assumption, assimilation, behavior, personality, cognition, intuition, awareness, etc.

After some debate, four successive trips deploying four Emulation-Vehicles were agreed upon as the optimum approach for several reasons.

Foremost, the decision was driven due to receptor-neuron acceptance-cycles. Difficult to manage due to sensory-neuron recovery proficiency is whether a "landing-zone" sensory-neuron would be in "on-state" upon 'touch-down': i.e., sensors are not always 'on' but go through 'on-off' refresh cycles. This characteristic also substantially varies by 'sensor-grid' in regards to a receptor-neurons required "rest-time" interval: so choosing the correct grid at the correct time is imperative.

Notably, if one of the specifically targeted sensors were in refresh 'off-state' upon arrival, the Emulation-Vehicle (EV) would bounce off, be absorbed into body fluid or simply dissipate as heat energy: this would not be good. Four vehicles will therefore provide needed redundancy: helping ensure a successful journey.

Responsively, to both maximize chances of successful acceptance and minimize the disaster-scenario occurrence, operational support went above and beyond by not only creating a sophisticated neural-detection / guidance system but also installing it as one of AIMs vast array of capabilities.

Thus, AIMs were well equipped to not only safeguard secure arrival on an active neuron but also accurately co-ordinate myriads of other technical complexities: such as, intercommunication and coordination between the four vehicles; and re-mimicking. Nicely, AIM has performed flawlessly during multiple training trials.

Notably, each EV will provide slightly-to-radically different views of 'trip' events. Although one proposed scenario posits the EVs will remain in close proximity during their 500 to 2000 millisecond (half-second to 2 second) sojourns; another suggests the quite likely possibility EVs will be slotted into different data-streams because some or all may be 'accepted' in different milliseconds.

Consequently, each would 'travel' independently and never be in each other's vicinity. Point is, until sufficient journey data is acquired, no-one can say for sure.

This brings us to the second reason for deploying four EVs instead of one. It is expected each EV will scoop enormous quantities of data. So whether EVs 'travel' together or apart, four 'virtual-travelers' viewing unfolding event in 'real-time' as if actually on an EV will be far superior to viewing one EVs data at a time and attempting to juggle it into the correct time sequence.

So, besides Cytoon and myself, Retic, the other two members of Team-1 are code named Mitoa and Vesi.

"I, Retic, am excited for this next journey because with this 'trip' we are for the first time in a technological position to not only experience each mechanism directly but also observe data-transition processes: thereby uncovering the intricacies and simplicities of how humans survive in this universes chaotic environment."

Mitoa, perhaps the most extreme of the T-1 group, is a brilliant physicist who prides himself on not being locked into one particular theory. He states, "Not only is Electromagnetism the fundamental building-block which drives how everything in our universe is organized but also, by the very nature of humans existing in this universe, forms the foundation, which defines how humans work as well".

Vesi is your non-stereotypical brain surgeon who insists the "brain" is a remarkable cross-system co-operative encompassing both Nervous and Endocrine systems. She states "there is no doubt our brain mass is intimately connected with each of the many, many thousands of external and internal sensory receptors and the accepted information is both 'frequency-identified' and 'intensity-graded' from the outset".

After all, encountered mechanisms in concert with 'sensory-data' are responsible for not only creating and modifying our physical and cognitive existence but also one's individual experience of reality.

Narrative Helpers

Journeys are expected to be exciting and complicated. To enhance clarity AIMs were provided flexible instruction-sets for not only gathering but also formatting and presenting data.

Opportunely, Cytoons previous research endeavors clarified EVs will encounter nine mechanisms, which will each uniquely deploy one-to-many "Filtering-and-Slotting" processes. More granularly, each process will also deploy specific steps to accomplish transforming inbound data-elements into mechanism mandated outbound configuration.

During planning it was determined consistent labeling of these three stratifications would definitely enhance understanding. Thus, "**Levels**" will be used indicate data-management mechanisms, which demarcate journey milestones; "**Stages**" will designate processes within a Level (mechanism); and "**Tasks**" will be used to demarcate deployed steps within a Stage.

Again due to Cytoons research, each expected Level (mechanism), Stage (processes within a mechanism) and Task (each step within a Stage) is able to be configured in a 'trip' outline. Containing brief descriptions, the "Soma-Self Self-Duo Milestones Guide" is located at DD-003 and will definitely enhance clarity.

It is also cross-referenced to the numbering on the 'Self-Duo' illustration (re-issued for convenience in larger form at DD-002 in the Detailed-Discussion segment).
I suggest bookmarking appropriate pages to keep them readily accessible because these items will be frequently referenced as the journey unfolds.

Now a little context has been provided, let's 'travel'.

Final Prep

I recall it was a very short debate, which decided the bombardment-event to emulate for this incredible first adventure. To honor the Black-Hole researchers whose work enabled Journey-One, each of the four Emulation-Vehicles will be configured to emulate a navel orange ester molecule: thus creating olfactory Deluge.

So as unglamorous as it might sound, the starting-point for our incredible journey will be by insertion of the EVs into an external burst of molecules and droplets generated by squishing an orange.

We are to be the smell, so to speak!

Cytoon promises the journey will not only surprise, excite and inform you but also provide perspectives capable of enhancing the enjoyment of your living journey!

Even though the actual journey will be of short duration (one-half to 2 seconds) the captured data will be immense. Consequently, when the 500 to 2000 millisecond journey is decoded into 'real-time', about 90 minutes of unparalleled intelligence about "How-We-Work" will be available for analysis.

Journey-One Begins

After the Emulation-Vehicles were recovered and reconstituted, each teammate prepared for AIMs virtual-rendering of individual EV journeys: beginning from "Out-There".

While settling into their designated DiHol gyroscopic chairs, headset chatter was bristling with anticipation about what might be uncovered while flowing along with a data-stream. Including the ground crews, everyone was excited to not only see how created technologies performed but also discover the many dynamic processes responsible for enabling our lives; our reality.

Out-There

Bombardment: Level 1: Stage 1 > Task 1

Suddenly airborne was the sensation a millisecond after Aymie, the designated member of our land-based support team, exuberantly crushed the chosen orange

Instantaneously, each Emulation-Vehicle was first miniaturized by its AIM (Artificial-Intelligence-Matrix) and then directed into the burst of millions of rapidly outward expanding ester molecules and droplets.

AIMs seamlessly infused each Emulation-Vehicle into the specific crop of molecules, previously calculated as most likely to impact the designated target: the nasal receptor grid of our volunteer: Big thanks to Ernie!

At surprisingly high velocity, my fellow researchers each reported approaching the small patch of neurons, which formed Ernie's target olfactory ('smell') receptors.

The shape of the Emulation-Vehicle, now mimicking an orange ester molecule was an acceptable 'fit' because I felt my EV lock into place, thanks to AIM moving and vibrating my "gyro-chair": definite proof my landing-zone was active upon touchdown and my EV presented the correct Tolerable-Signal.

All craft had arrived without rejection: first task complete!

Transition

Mitoa shared that event-horizon sensory-neurons provide the transition-points between 'Out-There' bombardment and ones "inner-world" of experiences. Unbelievably, he said, these extraordinary workhorses also possess the competency to morph a fundamental action component of our universe from mechanical energy to electrical potential. Mitoas next statement was startling: he said without this primary capability, nothing would exist to us: as there would be no sensory perception.

Soma-Sensors

Sensory-Acceptance: Level 2: Stage 1 > Task 1

We all knew from briefings that just landing on a neuron-receptor is insufficient to ensure its engagement. It is much fussier about "what it accepts into its sanctum": as will be evidenced, tried and true genetic-template requirements rule.

AIM wonderfully provides us with continual situational updates. For instance, two event-horizon conditions must be fulfilled for an EV to be 'accepted'. AIM displayed its rendering on my holographic 3D display.

My touchdown had satisfied two criteria: energetic enough to excite the neuron to fire, which AIM displayed as "Intensity-Sufficient"; plus molecular frequency or signal-type were within the neurons "Gradient-of-Acceptability", which AIM displayed as "Valid Format".

AIM also displayed the same messages under each of the other three EV identifiers, which recognized the pioneer 'traveler' code names. It is nice to have an EV called Retic: rather catchy I think.

A short pause occurred as my EVs arrival energy (Threshold-Potential) was sufficient to excite the neuron into action. Each member of the team excitedly reported AIM used chair motion and vibration to provide a simulated experience of this occurrence. Always nice to see excitement: even if it comes from a neuron!

I had to recall correct signal type is critical as well: for instance, the emulated orange ester would have no effect on hearing, as it would be outside auditory gradient-of-acceptability: in other words not in Valid-Format or outside Tolerable-Signal. To review the two integral processes, Tolerable-Signal and Threshold-Potential, necessary to accomplish 'acceptance' may I suggest rereading DD-001.

Transition to Tags

Vesi highlighted bombardment type and physiological dispositions both dictate acceptance. She stated: Even though massive numbers of impacts may occur, bombardment configuration, neuron readiness and bombardment energy dictate acceptance.

Vesi additionally flagged it is these inter-relating factors, which determine the quantity of neurons firing, and therefore in turn yields the initial indicator of "bombardment-intensity".

Vesi continued: A sensory-neuron has two states; it either 'fires' or it doesn't. When it does fire, impact energy is morphed to "wave-energy" or 'action-potential'. Importantly, she said, it is significant to future understanding to note wave-energy is the same for every firing event.

Definitely, Cytoon chimed in; physiologically there are a finite number of neurons, which are in the "fire-ready" state. Therefore, the number of neurons excited has direct correlation to impacts or "signal-concentration" but understandably cannot exceed the quantities of neurons available for acceptance during the duration of a few second "event-pulse".

Think of a neuron firing, she continued, as contributing a value of 'one'. Therefore, a hundred firings would be equal to a bombardment-intensity of one-hundred; a thousand, equal to 1,000; and so on.

Signal-concentration however is not Neuro-physiologically important Cytoon stated, until further up the processing chain where it will be thoroughly examined.

Yes, no question 'acceptance' is a big deal, I said. It is truly where the rubber-hits-the-road because it jumps the barrier from the random 'Out-There' to the accepted "In-Here".

However, I continued the assignment of fixed and immutable data-element identifiers called "Tags" is what forever not only captures the uniqueness of a data-element but also identifies it as belonging to a particular group.

Cytoon stated, 'Tags' in a most incredible fashion inform higher-processors about what type of data was accepted and its exact impact-zone: Even so sensors provide one additional morphing tidbit.

Tags: Level 2: Stage 1 > Task 2

Our Emulation-Vehicles (EVs) provided some great new high-tech toys. The one I was looking forward to checking out, when more complex data was available, was DiHol: the "three dimensional holographic imager". If AIM is able to successfully present external incidences up on DiHol's semi-transparent display-sphere to expectations, it will be the greatest heads-up display ever.

After acceptance Mitoa stated, energy conversion from mechanical into electrical potential (wave-energy) is ostensibly instantaneous. Initial electrical potential is determined by the inherent frequency of neurons within a 'landing-zone'. This foundational contribution is amazing because it forever identifies a data-elements 'acceptance-location' to every following mechanism. (See DD-001 for review of SLIDs)

After conversion was accomplished I was not disappointed. Sitting in my gyro-chair at the equidistant center of DiHol, I was in awe as DiHol displayed each of the other EVs as red dots on a slightly larger circular green background and my EV on a blue background: thereby marking each crafts SLID or Soma-Location-ID as individual but same.

In this way AIM informed 'travelers' all EVs had been accepted within the same 'landing-zone' and within the same relative time span of a few milliseconds. This was great news as we would be 'travelling' together!

Mitoa stated: it is incredibly synchronous a Soma-Location-ID's finely tuned electromagnetic frequency is immutable. He continued by saying, SLIDs thereby form a critical function to the many future evaluators along the route because they pinpoint the originating impact location.

> Mitoa suggested we parallel Soma-Location-ID to a receiving device: such as a cell phone. By design, he said, only one specific cell phone will recognize a specifically transmitted finely sliced frequency or electromagnetic signal as defined by its cell phone number. Therefore, he continued, from a pool of millions and millions of very similar signals bombarding each phone or receiver, only one cell phone is designed, can tune to or accept its particular finely sliced frequency.

Miraculously, Mitoa stated, it is the electromagnetic spectrum at the very foundation of our universe, which not only ensures each sufficiently variant signal or frequency performs independently or cannot mix or overlap with other signals but also as a consequence of this invariability is the glue tying everything in the universe together.

> Thousands of other red dots were also on the screen representing 'real' energy converted events (obviously the orange was very juicy). It was so very cool to be able to not only independently track the four of us among all the other accepted data-elements but also have the thrill of feeling imbedded in the unfolding adventure by chatting with and getting expert points-of-view from the other 'virtual-travelers'.

Very quickly though AIMs representation on DiHol simultaneously changed not only our four EVs from current red dot to a dark blue dot on a green background but also the thousands of others from red to blue. This however was not a surprise.

> Cytoon said, as is the case for every differing particle, unique vibrational properties must be accounted for to ensure transmitted information also satisfies the "what impacted" requirement.

So, she said, immediately after acceptance the target neuron provided the primary action-potential. Secondarily though, the olfactory neurons are additionally sensitive to molecular vibration, the orange-ester in our case and thus duly attenuate the primary action-potential into its ultimate SLID frequency. (Also review section on SLIDs if required: DD-001)

Mitoa added a physics perspective to Cytoons Neuro-physiological explanation by stating, as different particles are vibrationally diverse one from another, their particular atomic oscillations provide slightly adjusted attenuation to the locations neuron-frequency signature.

> In other words, the impact locations neuron-frequency signature gets re-vamped by incorporating a specific molecular vibrational signature. In this way orange 'smell' for instance can be discriminated from apple 'smell'; etc.

Cytoon suggested, from here on, accepted and attenuated bombardment simply be called "Tags".

Transition to Melding

Once attaining 'Tag' status then, we were whisked into a very small channel indeed.

Emulation-Vehicle 'landing' had occurred on an impossibly small neuron. There EVs were quickly accepted, energized and attenuated. Although for us Journey-One was a sight-seeing tour, the neuron was definitely all business.

Wasting no time, AIM displayed each Emulation-Vehicle, now 'Tags', being whisked away. Then AIM circled us around DiHol's sphere a few times: jumbled in with all the 'real' Tags of course. I thought I was going to give up some of my breakfast as the chair quickly swirled around to provide what AIM considered to be a representative experience. (Note to self: talk to the programmers.)

As my last rotation completed, AIM projected a transparent grid resembling a cornucopia on DiHol. AIM then dynamically twisted it overhead and 'pulled' it down over my head quickly filling the DiHol display surface until I was completely encased.

The experience was like being shunted into and rapidly traveling along a tiny pathway. Regardless of the scariness of the ride, fascinating was to observe the quantity of diverse Tags proportionately increase as the representation of the neural-pathway gradually began widening.

Amazing Emulation-Vehicle technology empowered each team member to truly feel they were independently coursing along on the wave-energy. However, it was AIMs depiction on DiHol which made this part of the journey unforgettable to me.

> As Emulation-Vehicles were rapidly carried along ever widening tributaries AIM really did make it feel like I was surfing a large wave through an ever enlarging tunnel: Definitely a fun part of the journey!

It was now becoming necessary to get friendly; very fast. Population in the smaller nerve channels, even though thousands of companion Tags (red dots) were present, seemed sparse by comparison to the significantly expanding populations in the larger conduits. When I shared this with the others they all agreed.

> Vesi chimed in by stating it is expected as tributaries widen, Tag type varieties will grow proportionately. She stated this is because Tags were being added exponentially from multitudes of other Soma-Location-ID's (SLIDs) situated all over external and internal event-horizons.

AIM depicted all activity by displaying a body outline complete with nervous-system encompassing about half DiHol's surface. Within this displayed framework, AIM then presented Tags as popping up at thousands of sensory locations by encoding them with different shapes and colors. Tags were depicted as flowing along smaller nerve channels and into main neural-branches everywhere: the massive bustle was mesmerizing.

> Vesi thought depictions of Tags as different shapes and colors to define uniquely attenuated Tag-frequencies as each originating from different Soma-Location-IDs, extraordinary. She also thought something else was now very clear. To experience journeys from each originating Tag location (SLID) will require thousands of trips: Everyone exuberantly chimed in they were on-board to try them all.

Wave-Bands: Level 2: Stage 1 > Task 3

As lots of other 'Tag-traffic' as well as my EV arrived in the main branch, it quickly slotted into the next flowing layer or "wave-band". I found it appealing wave-bands were initially depicted by AIM on DiHol like sheets in a pad of paper, except the sheets were thicker and transparent.

By showing thousands of different shapes and colors within each 'sheet' boundary, AIM made it obvious Tags within our designated 'wave-band' had coalesced as a result of tens-of-thousands of active neurons accepting and 'Tagging' bombardment-events within the same few millisecond acceptance window.

So whether Tags were similar or widely variant, originally physically close or extremely remote, they were destined to hitch-a-ride in the next "time-sliced" wave-band.

> Cytoon added a 'wave-band' with its randomly distributed 'captured' Tags endures as a cohesive unit: in other words, neither the wave-band nor its 'Tag-residents' intermingle with the Tags of other wave-bands. Critically, she continued, this strategy ensures event "time-slices" remain cohesive: i.e., stable wave-band snippets rigidly maintain the integrity of close 'timeline-common' bombardment event occurrences. Implications will be discussed further along, Cytoon inserted.

AIM quickly redisplayed the moving wave-band 'paper-pad' into what resembled a very elongated Ferris-wheel.

This representation made two other characteristics obvious: each 'Ferris-wheel' seat (wave-band) was identically spaced and equidistant each from the next; and the Ferris-wheel 'speed' and therefore wave-band pace was constant. I suggested and all agreed the wave-band structure was no doubt functioning as a exceptional "flow-regulator".

Melding: Level 2: Stage 1 > Task 4

It was fun to be part of and observe the myriads of 'Tags-of-like-frequencies' coalescing or melding into assemblages. To depict the amalgamation phenomenon AIM first cluttered DiHol with about a dozen kinds of birds spattered in a virtual blue sky then quickly, as if a whistle blew, flocked each species into discrete migratory formations: Melding is obviously incredibly swift.

Straightaway though, AIM faded the above 'flocks' image and constructed up on DiHol a new image of 99 trailing wave-bands plus ours to look like a much enlarged deck of cards. However, the 'cards' were variously hued, transparent and quite thick.

In order to show wave-bands at different stages of melding AIM quickly morphed the 'cards' display by separating the 100 wave-band 'cards' and fanning them out around DiHol's sphere. Incredibly within our wave-band, which AIM showed much larger, many hundreds of variously sized 'melded-groups' were now present: each displaying different shapes and colors.

AIM vigorously rotated my chair to show their distribution beginning from lower left (farthest away), wrapping overhead and ending with our wave-band on the lower right: spellbinding! (Except, to not end upside down would be nice: additional note for programmers).

> Cytoon elaborated by saying once Tags of like kind merge the resulting 'melded-groups' are redesignated "Tag-Clusters" or "TCs".

One other feature was also obvious: all wave-band dimensions were identical. I postulated this was AIMs way of indicating all wave-bands provide identical capacity. Also apparent some wave-bands contained more 'Tag-Clusters'; some less.

Understandably, I conjectured, variance was partially due to not only the extreme activity caused by the 'orange-squishing' but also our volunteer Ernie's excitement, which provided heightened neuron acceptance activity.

Very definitively, to provide a percentage indication of wave-band utilization, AIM posted a number in the visible corner of each wave-band: ours was 41, the highest; the lowest utilization percent was 23. Constructively, utilization percentage not only provides a relative indicator of bombardment activity but also proofs fluctuations occur continually as highlighted by the range of indicated values.

Mitoa eagerly commented it will be fascinating to observe how follow-on mechanisms handle 'normal' as well as extreme fluctuations.

Additionally though, I noticed same type Tag-Clusters, observable due to common color and shape, varied substantially in 'size' (a physical dimension attribute AIM used to indicate variances in Tag-Cluster wave-potential) across the 100 wave-bands. For instance, our Tag-Cluster in our wave-band was much larger than its comparative, which hitched-a-ride 90 wave-bands later.

Vesi thought the variance, due to our created Deluge events short acceptance duration, was nicely underlined when AIM faded out all the other types of Tag-Clusters in all wave-bands. It was ideal she said because by looking down the line at the 99 following wave-bands, it was easy to spot the reduction in Tag-Cluster size.

Cytoon quickly pointed out the 'size' decrease, representing a decline in action-potential, was due to the corresponding decline in neuron-acceptance for our olfactory bombardment event as orange ester concentration also faded at our SLID.

Inception-Filter

> Arrival at Inception-Filter, the first Soma-Self mechanism: so far, so good!

Aptly framed-up on DiHol's display, AIM again made it clear our inbound wave-band arrived at "Inception-Filter" with all Tags melded into segregated homogenous Tag-Cluster groups. AIM made two other characteristics obvious by its detailed displays: the Ferris-wheel 'seats' (wave-bands) were continually and regularly arriving; and wave-bands not only delivered substantially varied Tag-Cluster populations but also Tag-Cluster fluctuations across and within wave-bands were in direct correlation to volatile Deluge.

> Now evident to me, Inception-Filter is one busy place. Like a rivers flow is sustained by hundreds of creeks, Inception-Filters persistent action is instigated by the flow of regularly arriving wave-bands: one every three milliseconds, which deciphers to about 333 per minute.

To clearly depict inbound to Inception-Filter structure, AIM adroitly reconfigured our wave-band by presenting it on DiHol as a large transparent ball with hundreds of other spherical objects of different shapes, colors and sizes, representing Tag-Clusters, suspended as if weightless within its confines. Conspicuously, lots of room remained as our wave-band Tag-Clusters only occupied about 41% of capacity.

> To enhance clarity, AIM displayed the above 'Soma-Self' illustration. Provided by Cytoon it depicts layered Soma-Self mechanisms and processes. I was happy to see this distinctive format, which nicely compliments the Self-Duo illustration located in the Detailed-Discussion segment at DD-002.

To kick off next steps, Cytoon informed us, after an inbound wave-band is discharged into Inception-Filters 'in-box', two stages are sequentially expedited: hierarchical organization of Tag-Clusters; then broadcasting to "Soma-Cluster".

Ranking: Level 2: Stage 2 > Task 1

AIM wasted no time demonstrating the "ranking-stage". On DiHol AIM displayed the rapid sorting of our wave-band Tag-Clusters into single file. AIM made obvious the 'largest' or 'greatest-potential' Tag-Cluster was positioned first; the next largest, second; and so forth until all were sequenced.

> AIMs rendering of the hierarchical process on DiHol was excellent. AIM stretched and molded DiHols current 'ball' display into a long transparent tapering tube. Within this 'tube' were displayed thousands of variously shaped, colored and sized spherical objects, representing Tag Clusters, stacked one behind the other: from 'largest' to 'smallest' with our Tag-Cluster in the first position. It was ingenious the way AIM also ensured EVs were easy to spot within our Tag-Cluster by blinking our four tiny red dots.

Mitoa put a physics spin on renderings by additionally explaining the stratification process. It is actually a consequence of universal laws, he said, which dictate the dominance of higher electrical potentials across biological membranes.

Although proofing is beyond scope at this point he stated, feel free to investigate the characteristics of both 'electric potential energy' and 'electrostatic potential energy' at your convenience. For future reference I noted these suggestions as I have many others on my AIM voice-recognition idea-pad.

> This makes sense Vesi said, as the highest activity bombardment locations (SLIDs), as indicated by the 'largest' Tag-Clusters, should get addressed first. Very limited neural-real-estate and processors, she continued, are best utilized by first handling higher-intensity ('larger' Tag-Clusters) and thus possible survival-critical issues. As a reminder, she added, a Tag-Cluster is 'bigger' due to the SLIDs Tag count being 'larger' she said because of greater quantities of neurons simultaneously accepting Deluge at an event-horizon.

Broadcasting: Level 2: Stage 2 > Task 2

AIMs simulation of this task felt similar to being shot from cannon. Our Tag-Cluster was being energetically shunted along what appeared like a transparent pipe. No doubt I and the others were being pulled toward Soma-Cluster to our ultimate "Matched-Base-Frequency" destination.

I knew from Cytoons trial-run briefings Soma-Cluster was comprised of thousands of genetically inspired Matched-Base-Frequency arrays. It will be interesting to observe Tag-Clusters 'hooking-up'.

Cytoon proceeded by explaining the "broadcasting-stage" propagates the hierarchically organized wave-potentials toward appropriate brain-mass: in this case toward Soma-Cluster neural-arrays. Broadcast ensures a Tag-Cluster has sufficient energy-resources to 'arrive' at the correct Matched-Base-Frequency data-resource.

Upon arrival she added "Recognition-Assessment" will engage to first determine "recognition-status" then depending on assessment outcome, either dispatch to "Threat-Check" or "Intensity-Assessment".

Just after Broadcast, AIM rendered our Tag-Cluster wave-band on DiHol as dissipating. By spawning thin irregular waving lines to indicate energy pulsations, AIM confirmed residual wave-band energy was indeed responsible for nudging each Tag-Cluster toward Soma-Cluster.

I thought the representation of liberating our wave-band Tag-Clusters by AIM was fascinating. AIM interwove and swirled our EVs, as well as the other Tag-Clusters, which were once 'travelling' in our wave-band, around the upper semi-sphere of DiHol's display. This representation effectively simulated attraction toward Soma-Cluster and ultimately entering specific Matched-Base-Frequency compatible arrays.

It was quite a ride as AIM in synch with its display rocked and moved my chair to 'avoid' the other Tag-Clusters.

Quickly though AIM changed the 'open-spaces' representation into a dynamic experience by gyrating my chair and displaying EVs as rapidly moving along ever narrowing tubes. AIM dodged my EV this way or that as each of the myriads of branching neural intersections, into which other Tag-Clusters flowed, were encountered.

At this point Cytoon surprised us by disclosing a really excellent journey alternate had been planned. She informed us that three of the craft had been successfully programed to be 'UN-recognized' and 'high-intensity' thus directing the Tag-Cluster toward the Threat-Check path from Recognition-Assessment. Conversely, the remaining EV would be directed to "Soma-Slotting" by being 'recognized and 'low-intensity'.

So Mitoa, she said, as you are destined for Soma-Slotting, we are all going to change our AIMs to experience your journey first and then afterwards all travel the Threat-Check path as well.

As evidenced by the positive chatter this was a welcome revelation because although unspoken until now Vesi, Mitoa and I were thinking we would be missing a journey alternate.

Recognition-Assessment: Level 2: Stage 2 > Task 3

At this point Cytoon requested a few minutes to inform regarding what to expect next.

Cytoon began by suspending AIM and adding the 'Matched-Base-Frequency' graphic as shown below to the existing 'Soma-Self' illustration launched earlier. Please take a moment to check-out the additional illustration I just put up on DiHol, Cytoon suggested, as it will be used to coordinate discussions.

Cytoon then followed-up by saying as everyone can see from the illustration as presented on your display (below), the next journey portion will involve "Recognition-Assessment". Notably integral to Inception-Filter, she continued, Recognition-Assessment provides a critical evaluation: namely, identification of an inbound Tag-Cluster as either "recognized" or 'problematic'.

'Problematic' is definitely determined when a Tag-Cluster is "UN-recognized" by its Matched-Base-Frequency, Cytoon elaborated. In this situation the Tag-Cluster is immediately replicated.

Whereas the replicated Tag-Cluster is utilized to initialize and populate the Matched-Base-Frequency data-archive, the original Tag-Cluster is shunted to Threat-Check for further analysis.

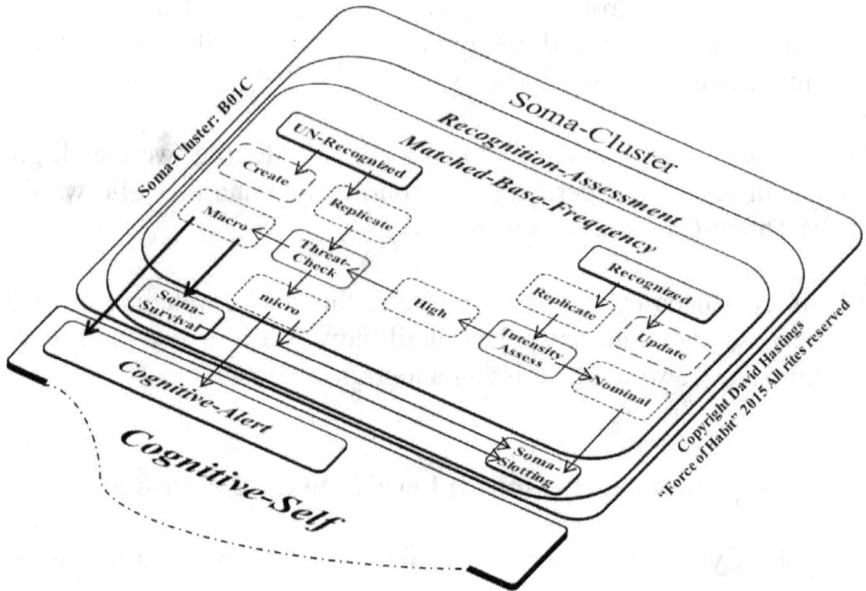

Such quick handling of unknown situations has huge ramifications for our species as it enables us to quickly adapt to a broad range of situations: and therefore survive.

I'm sure, Vesi said, everyone realizes UN-recognized events, like being in a cage with an agitated wild tiger, pose the greatest threat and stress.

Vesi substantiated her proposition by stating this is so because when data-archives necessary for both comparison and appropriate action are not available one invariably and appropriately feels lost and fearful: perhaps even 'frozen' to the spot; unable to move. Indubitably, she said, due to lack of response-foddering data-archives, response-actions will be ineffective and/or inappropriate.

Definitely, Cytoon agreed recognized or previously 'Bracketed' events do contribute most of the fodder. Interestingly on the flip-side though, she continued when experience is great, like playing a favorite sport for years, substantial similar sensory input has filled-out or substantially incremented the action-potentials of appropriate data-archives.

Therefore, the new sensory-event, if sufficiently intense, only provides the spark to instigate Threat-Check and Cognitive-Self alerts; whereas data-archives provide the bulk of the information utilized by Soma-Response patterning, which I will discuss more extensively further along.

Resultantly, Recognition-Assessment plays a vital role Vesi added. As an inbound Tag-Cluster is received at its Matched-Base-Frequency in Soma-Cluster data-repository, due to Inception-Filters broadcast, Recognition-Assessment first determines if the inbound Tag-Cluster frequency is 'recognized' (exact match) or 'UN-recognized' (blank Matched-Base-Frequency data-resource).

In other words, the target Matched-Base-Frequency is either populated or not.

Actually, Soma-Self neural-resources are very sparse when compared to Cognitive-Self, Vesi continued. Hence, the implication for dichotomous determination at this juncture also sustains effective resource usage: 'recognized' will not usurp as many neural-resources as will 'un-recognized'.

Notably, she continued 'UN-recognized' will require additional processing-resources to immediately "Bracket" or archive the Tag-Cluster: i.e., instill or Bracket the UN-recognized Tag-Cluster into its dedicated Matched-Base-Frequency data-resource. Consequently, she stated Bracketing is critical for fast response because it establishes Tag-Clusters, which will therefore be 'recognized' when again encountered.

Recognition-Assessment provides obvious value Cytoon agreed. She inserted its strategies are the first step to enabling recognition to drive appropriate "Response-Pattern" selection, which ultimately results in force appropriate habitual "Soma-Action": a future topic she noted.

Vesi confirmed only two outbound channels are possible from Recognition-Assessment: Threat-Check or Intensity-Assessment. Resultantly she reiterated ultimate conduit determination is inter-dependent on two characteristics: recognition and/or intensity.

Bracketing: Level 3: Stage 1 > Task 2

As AIM panned the 'outside' landscape, thousands of neurons intertwined branches and trunks of differing lengths filled the visual-scape way into the distance. It was like actually being inside the brain and looking out on the vista from the perspective of being 'very-tiny': incredible!

Quite suddenly, when only our EVs and the 'real' Tag members remained, AIM changed the display to a shimmering pale blue, which signals, Cytoon indicated, not only arrival at but also 'recognition' by our Matched-Base-Frequency. In other words, we were not the first orange ester to arrive at this Matched-Base-Frequency.

Replication: Level 3: Stage 1 > Task 1

Almost simultaneously to my observation of AIMs rendition, our Tag-Cluster, like some kind of cellular division, became two: our Tag-Cluster had just been replicated.

Then fluidly, like a creek peacefully entering a lake, AIM showed the cloned Tag-Cluster blending with the pool of blue. It had just been absorbed into its Matched-Base-Frequency data-archive: therefore becoming one with volunteer Ernie's 'frequency-memory' Bracket.

At this point Cytoon suspended AIMs presentation to explain what had just occurred. She stated although EV emulation fooled the mechanisms to date our EVs were not the required exact match to Matched-Base-Frequency and therefore our four EVs, although still part of the original Tag-Cluster, were omitted when replication occurred.

> Good news for two reasons she continued because Matched-Base-Frequency replication precision ensures not only will no spurious bits, think of them as contaminants, became archived but also serious difficulties arising, if the EVs had been cloned, were avoided.

If you would like more detailed information regarding Neuro-physiological functioning of Recognition-Assessment evaluation methodology as well as explanation of Axon Terminal/Dendrite Pathways, Bracketing, Soma-

Cluster and Matched-Base-Frequencies, Vesi said please access DD-004 information.

Intensity-Assessment: Level 3: Stage 1 > Task 3

'Problematic', as with 'UN-recognized' Tag-Clusters, can also be true Cytoon alerted, when a 'recognized' Tag-Cluster "intensity-gradient" exceeds its Matched-Base-Frequencies "nominal-range".

> It is important to note there may still be a threat even though Tag-Clusters are recognized. A firefighter may be familiar with procedures to fight the inferno all around him but no doubt will be on high survival alert with his 'Intensity-Assessment' working at max to navigate and avoid marginal survival situations.

So regardless of 'recognized-status', the original Tag-Cluster is always fired to "Intensity-Assessment" for further evaluation. The replicant on the other hand as per the Matched-Base-Frequency illustration is utilized to update or expand the action-potential of its Matched-Base-Frequency data-resource.

In summary then, Cytoon stated, 'UN-recognized **and/or** high-intensity' as shown on the Soma-Self illustration derives from two Recognition-Assessment evaluation streams. Cytoon cautioned to note the 'and/or' because 'UN-recognized' will immediately trigger both Threat-Check and Cognitive-Alert; and perhaps "Survival-Threat" processes.

> Differently, 'recognized' employs Intensity-Assessment, which engages Threat-Check only when it determines 'amplified-intensity'.

Conversely, Cytoon said, 'recognized' **and** 'low-intensity' (stress on the 'and' without the 'or') is much less neural-resource demanding because data-archiving can be handled by Recognition-Assessment without the need for either Treat-Check survivability assessment or rousing Cognitive-Self for assistance.

Nominal Channel

>Cytoon reminded as previously discussed, 'recognized-and-low-intensity' is the currently designated avenue.

I think the science teams responsible for AIM technologies are to once again be congratulated for also developing program instruction-sets to reconfigure an Emulation-Vehicles "mimic-halo" on-route, I said.
Yes Vesi concurred; re-mimicking capability effectively allows an EV to be specifically 'directed' to the desired channel.

>Vesi pointed out a fun fact: our journey duration in the 'real' world would have been about one-third of a second: fast, she said, does not begin to describe it.

Soma-Slotting: Level 3: Stage 2 > Task 1

For instance, for this leg of our journey, Mitoas EV mimic-halo was reconfigured as 'recognized-and-intensity-nominal' upon arrival at the target Matched-Base-Frequency. Thereby, Intensity-Assessment after ratifying Mitoas Emulation-Vehicle as intensity-nominal catapulted it to "Soma-Slotting".

Upon arrival at the Soma-Slotting 'in-box' the environment was peaceful: but not for long. To characterize the goings-on, AIM presented a scene on DiHol suggestive of a train station.

When AIM showed our Emulation-Vehicle arriving at the 'stations' exterior, all was calm. However, as AIM virtually escorted us through its 'doors', external-tranquility quickly changed to internal-bustle.

>AIMs portrayal reminded me of a trip I took a few years back from New York to Boston on the first day of spring-break: 'never-again' lesson learned. Everything looked fine when the taxi dropped me off at 'arrivals', however as soon as I stepped through the doors hundreds-and-hundreds of jostling people were either drifting about or lining up at airline kiosks.

Intensity: Nominal

AIM, as it did during the 'Ranking-task' earlier, seamlessly converted the DiHol scene to now depict 'station-people' as variously shaped, colored and sized spheres. Immediately noticeable was one big difference: whereas previous spheres, representing Tag-Clusters, were vastly different sizes; the surrounding spheres were not. Actually, all were about the same size and rather smallish.

Vesi said AIMs presentation was consistent for Soma-Slotting "working-data" because 'larger' or higher-intensity Tag-Clusters, regardless of whether 'recognized' or not were directed to Threat-Check. The outcome, she stated, is Soma-Slotting Tag-Clusters, regardless of diversity, present limited "intensity-range" action-potentials, which of course AIM represents as 'size'. Stated differently she said only 'intensity-nominal' Tag-Clusters arrive at Soma-Slotting.

> Remember, Cytoon reiterated, our EV was enabled to take this journey spur because the Emulation-Vehicles 'mimic-halo' was specifically adjusted by AIM to coincide with the 'size' characteristic necessary for Intensity-Assessment to determine 'intensity-nominal' and thus spit us into the Soma-Slotting 'in-box'.

Soma-Slotting In-Box

Another aspect of our situation seems glaring though, I said: the Soma-Slotting 'in-box' is obviously a gathering place; not a conduit for rapid outbound handover. Just as I finished speaking AIM changed the 'kiosks' display into a familiar structure utilized previously: an elongated Ferris-Wheel.

> Now I get it I said: to limit capacity and to ensure 'time-slice' data-integrity "Flow-Bands" are again used.

Yes, Vesi said, AIMs rendition provides confirmation of what was expected: "Selective-Amalgamation". Recall she said the first wave-band securely delivered sensory Tag-Clusters to Inception-Filter in a time-sliced group called a wave-band.

Subsequently, Recognition-Assessment released Tag-Clusters from wave-band influence and propagated each toward Soma-Cluster purposed to locate their specific Matched-Base-Frequency.

Only after effectively breaking up initial wave-band groupings, does Soma-Cluster processing initiate Recognition-Assessment, Cytoon offered. Its evaluators potentially direct some Tag-Clusters, evaluated as 'UN-recognized' and 'high-intensity' toward the "Unrecognized-Channel" and ultimately Threat-Check.

Alternately, she continued, Recognition-Assessment flushes the balance, the 'recognized' Tag-Clusters, toward the "Recognized-Channel" and ultimately Intensity-Assessment, which determines and shunts either 'problematic' to Threat-Check or 'nominal' to Soma-Slotting.

Resultantly, Vesi stated, Tag-Clusters are effectively being filtered into different 'time-slices' as a consequence of variable processor "action-timeframes". Critically, she added, regardless of channel Soma-Slotting is the destination for all but the highest-intensity Tag-Clusters, which are handled by Survival-Threat instead.

> Therefore, she suggested, understanding Soma-Slotting's Filtering-and-Slotting process is critical because it sets the stage for appreciating the necessity of 'Selective-Amalgamation', which will impact following processes considerably.

Recognition-Assessment then, Vesi summarized, selectively slots applicable Tag-Clusters to Threat-Check while others are destined for Intensity-Assessment. However, she elaborated, once a Tag-Cluster shoots from its Matched-Base-Frequency, subsequent grouping with other Tag-Clusters is a necessity.

> Incredibly, she said in an astonished tone, many thousands per millisecond concurrently emerge from both 'unrecognized' and 'recognized' channels and get rushed to Soma-Slotting, which is unenviably charged with handling this copious filtered onslaught.

Wave-band regulators, purposed to avoid overload by capping capacity and thereby controlling "data-flow", Vesi stated operate as a "transfer-mechanism" throughout "neural-arenas".

Critically, she added, survival mandates would not be well served if Tag-Clusters were allowed to propagate to following Levels, Stages or Tasks willy-nilly.

Instead, gathering and re-grouping emerged Tag-Clusters into an action 'time-slice' within a mechanism specific wave-band provides far superior continuity.

Interface to the OUT-THERE

I would like to provide clarity regarding ultimate purpose, Cytoon jumped in. The channel we are 'travelling' as well as the others has a final mandate: interface with the real-world via triggering Soma-Actions.

In other words, she rephrased, outcome will be some physical movement. Consequently, somatic actions, no matter how small, will almost certainly initiate sensory-feedback, which will arrive at Inception-Filter thus continuing a loop, which continues for a lifetime.

Although a difficult accomplishment, Cytoon submitted, for Soma-Actions to effectively enhance survival-potential, they absolutely must be in temporal alignment with the multitudes of accepted sensory-events, which initiated them.

It would just not do to stub your toe and respond by scratching your nose; or swinging your tennis racket in the wrong direction long after the ball passed. Therefore, she added specific coordination between "sensory-impetus" and "responsive-actions" is essential.

> I find incredible our flowing Bombardment-Sphere interactions with the Out-There are even possible Cytoon said: especially when considering the massive and rapid flow as well as all the many Filtering-and-Slotting processes necessary for evaluation, realignment and action. For instance, take a look at the short requirements list I have displayed at coordinates DD-005.

Not just that, Vesi interjected, but the sensory-events from which Soma-Action patterns its responses must not only stem from an appropriate time-frame but also address as many discrete sensory-events across a target time-snippet as possible.

> In other words, if you stubbed your toe while falling down the stairs multiple conditions need to be addressed; whereas the bumping of your head a couple of minutes ago should not enter the evaluation picture.

Therefore, Vesi said, to be of any use, although Deluge is random and Tag-Clusters discrete due to SLID origins, response must be tightly coordinated to sensory-acceptance locations and timeline. Unacceptable and ineffective would be random responses to each individual SLID.

What will work however is coordinated 'outbounds' effecting responses in proportion to SLID intensity as captured within appropriate flowing 'time-slices', modulated by honeable "pattern-brackets".

> Can you imagine Mitoa chuckled, if each SLID required individual response…what a jerky mess that would cause!

Definitely Cytoon said but your humorous observation highlights the first purpose of Soma-Slotting: to ensure sufficient but not extraneously large quantities of 'working-data' are correctly grouped. Secondly, but no less important she continued, the Soma-Slotting mandate is to format selected grouping into an effective "multiple-concurrent" form, which Soma-Response can quickly accept and evaluate.

Selective-Amalgamation thus affords two benefits: a superior data cross-section for Soma-Response pattern initiation as discussed above; and an elegant means of slowing the information flow into the physical world second-by-second timeframe from the millisecond timeframe employed by the Neuro-physiological acceptance, transfer and evaluation environments.

Slotting-Template

As if somehow listening, I didn't know if I should be in awe or a little afraid, AIM morphed the now familiar elongated Ferris-Wheel 'kiosk' as well as the 'waiting-area' DiHol displays into something quite different.

The 'waiting-area', became a transparent rectangular cube with an end wall completely utilized by thousands of regularly spaced small openings of different shapes and colors.

> Made obvious by the way AIM morphed the DiHol display, these openings were the previous few generic kiosks: except now thousands were present and all were unique.

Augmenting this scene, AIM displayed thousands of spheres of different shapes and colors, some even the same, as floating within the remaining area of the 'waiting-area'. As AIM zoomed in on a small section of the "kiosk-wall" it was evident to me identical shape and color spheres were being quickly drawn into their shape and color compatible "kiosk-receptor".

Then at regular intervals the entire 'kiosk-wall' array was contiguously launched out the back-end. In a very short 300 millisecond timeframe, as displayed on DiHol by AIM, I watched this fixed-interval cycle exactly repeat many times: drawing in Tag-Clusters from the 'waiting-area'; then after a consistent time-cycle, launching the 'kiosk-wall' out the other end.

> Also incredible was the scene when I looked back into the 'waiting-area' because new 'spheres' or Tag-Clusters were continually arriving and nudging previous ones forward.

I totally appreciated the next presentation AIM deposited on DiHol, as well. AIM zoomed in close to the first kiosk-receptor on the top left then quickly travelled the top row going right, then the second row going left and weaved its way all the way through thousands to the last kiosk-receptor.

Inspiring was what AIM was doing as it was moving along the rows. As AIM arrived at each kiosk-receptor it sounded a musical tone, which escalated ever-so-slightly one to the next: from lowest at the first kiosk-receptor to highest at the last.

Thus, by utilizing exceedingly small frequency increments to distinguish kiosk-receptor, was not only the sequenced sound incredible but also clear each kiosk-receptor actually represented a Soma-Location-ID or SLID.

> I could not resist sharing an observation with the group. I am astonished, I said because by AIM traversing back-and-forth across the 'kiosk-wall' array, does not only each two row segment describe a wave but also the end-to-end voyage a sinusoidal repeating wave. I appreciated the ooo's and ahh's.

Cytoon was very excited as she shared are not only kiosk-receptors designed for specific SLIDs but also 'spheres' their matching Tag-Clusters of sensory origin. What amazing symmetry from sensory-acceptance to Soma-Slotting; which, as an aside, turns out to be well named.

I have observations perhaps someone can explain: I noticed two frequent occurrences: not all kiosk-receptors had 'sphere' occupants at 'launch-time' and sometimes kiosk-receptors attracted and accommodated many of the same shape and color 'spheres'.

It is however obvious thanks to AIM the kiosk-receptors as a whole array definitely perform as a wave-band: although incredibly specialized.

'Kiosk-Receptor' Populating

Vesi jumped in and said this is a perfect time to bring those points up; and yes 'very specialized' is a good way of putting it. With AIMs help I can explain as we unravel the reason for 'launch'; as well as its consequences.

In response to the first part of your question Retic, it is normal kiosk-receptors do not all get populated. This is so because 'sphere' availability is based on Bombardment and therefore not all SLIDs are activated all the time. She added one would hope one-hundred percent activation would never occur because the result would be total system overwhelm.

The second observation about many of the same 'spheres' being drawn into their compatible kiosk-receptor, Vesi offered, has to do with several factors: slowing down data-flow the millisecond-by-millisecond "neural-acceptance world" to the second-by-second "response-world"; acquiring multiple 'time-slices' for broader-scope or sensory-event collating; and for appropriate broader-scope 'time-slices', compounding the action-potentials or intensity of 'kiosk' compatible Tag-Clusters.

To summarize, Vesi continued, all mechanisms perform five functions to various extents: receive a previous mechanisms morphed data-stream, 'Filter' or re-characterize it according to fixed rules, potentially populate data-archives, 'Slot' or reconfigure and then send it outbound for the next mechanism to pick up and process.

Notably, she conceded Soma-Slotting runs the same functional processes: however it's outbound is unique. She added Soma-Slotting's clear mandate is to transform the data-stream in a way, which will create a 'best-case' outbound, which not only coordinates multiple sensory-receptions to applicable time-frames but also enables rapid and consistent physical interactions with the 'Out-There'. Definitely no minor task-set, she concluded.

The 'kiosk-wall' has one other characteristic, which comes into play big time, Cytoon interjected; it actually forms a pattern or template as its kiosk-receptor order never changes. Therefore, the outbound will always present SLIDs in a consistent pattern. However, that being said, one other factor, besides Tag-Cluster diversity, remains variable: our old friend intensity she fervently added.

Kiosk-Harmonic

With Cytoons disclosure, I will not keep you in suspense any longer, Vesi said: the "first-layer" output from Soma-Slotting is not going to be a 'simple-frequency' but a "complex-harmonic" derived from all the simple 'sphere' frequencies, which were loaded into and launched from the 'kiosk-wall': Let's call the 'first-layer' outbound creation a "Kiosk-Harmonic", Vesi suggested.

> Actually, Vesi added, the outcome is not unlike what we experience every day when we listen to music.

Let me suggest, Vesi said, the metamorphosis from individual 'simple' frequencies to a blended 'complex' harmonic can be likened to experiencing a Symphony Orchestra for the first time.

Let's assume, she continued you arrive at a performance about thirty minutes early. Accordingly, you are just in time to share in the orchestras warming up phase. Although there are many identifiable sounds, she elaborated, the cacophony, due to all sorts of random noises without pattern is not so agreeable.

Actually, Vesi chortled the uninitiated could easily wonder how anything useable could come from such disjointed racket. However, she said random noises instantly change when the conductor taps his baton and inspires all the diverse components to come into synchronicity.

> Suddenly harmonies, which are not only beautifully cohesive but also wonderfully variant, resonate with our genetically encoded frequency receptors so strongly one also senses or feels connected to the foundation of 'How-We-Work': sometimes to tears, Vesi said.

Additionally, Vesi cheerfully added sometimes one or a group of instruments are louder or more 'intense'; at different times other instruments take the spotlight. This analogy she added is consistent because as multiple 'same-type' Tag-Clusters or 'spheres' entering a kiosk before launch immediately amalgamate, they resultantly form a larger action-potential or higher-intensity: like blowing a trumpet louder. Of course, she reminded us most of the other drawn-in Tag-Cluster intensities also vary one from the next.

Orchestras, Vesi concluded use one methodology as building blocks for designing patterned and mixed frequency combinations or harmonic effects – notes and instruments: Living species utilize another; frequencies and genetics. As nearly limitless music possibilities arise from combining 12 fundamental music notes, she stated, imagine the harmonic combinations enabled by genetics utilizing many thousands of SLID frequencies.

Thus, Cytoon said, the particular expanded 'time-sliced' thousands of Tag-Cluster frequencies with all their potential combinations and variant intensities, which were drawn into the 'kiosk-wall', were morphed by Soma-Slotting on 'launch' into a distinct harmonic tone or Kiosk-Harmonic. It is as identifiable to following processes she continued as the first strum or two of a familiar tune is to us.

In fact I will provide an example Cytoon said. One is able recognize a song pattern from a very few notes even when played by a different group using different instruments and arrangement. Actually, a few famous game shows employed this principal.

For example, Cytoon explained a few notes would be played and if one had ever heard the music from which the excerpt was extracted, one would recognize it immediately. Interestingly, getting the instrumental portion of the tune is a Soma-Self process; whereas dredging up the name is a job for Cognitive-Self.

> Cytoon excitedly added not surprising one recognizes simple to complex sounds very easily. Genetically we are all about frequencies and vibrations she augmented, across the expanse from atoms to molecules to compounds to organisms to 'brackets', frequencies are the common linking factor.

Mitoa our team Physicist added, it is not a big leap to expect genetic patterning to utilize the same Electromagnetic Frequency protocols as everything else in the universe. Communication and recognition by frequency are absolutely fundamental to all that goes on in, and around us.

The Electromagnetic Spectrum is the same feeder box for both corporeal manifestation and non-corporeal existence. Vibration is frequency; is sound; is electromagnetism: it is THE universal binding law; the basis of 'How-We-Work'.

Have you ever wondered Mitoa asked why sound in the form of some form of music has always been an integral part of human history? Its spontaneous universal appeal should not be surprising now we have come to understand vibration forms the very essence of who we are: our atoms vibrate; our molecules vibrate; our genetics vibrate; our tissues vibrate; the universe vibrates…

We are in sync!

Kiosk-Patterns

The "second-layer" output from Soma-Slotting Vesi said is not built for quick matching by Soma-Response, which will be discussed next, but for critical deployment by Soma-Action of SLID implicated 'Kiosk-Harmonic' connections to the 'Out-There' physical world.

As Vesi was speaking, AIM once again provided a clearly detailed three-dimensional display. It rotated the 'kiosk-wall' angling it at about thirty degrees from slightly below from the room or 'loading-end' view to the opposite side or the 'launching-end' view. AIM then proceeded to show Tag-Cluster launch as 'spires' of colored nearly transparent lines of different thicknesses and lengths launching from populated kiosk-receptors.

Next, AIM slowly rotated the transparent depiction, which clearly showed although the 'spires' at the launch-end were all in perfect alignment; lengths at the other end were various. Then AIM attached a thin transparent greenish-colored base-plate on the launch-end, which mirrored the kiosk-wall.

Resultantly it was obvious over half of the 'kiosk-wall' origination-points of this "Kiosk-Pattern" were without 'spires' meaning the applicable 'kiosk-receptor' was empty at time of 'launch'. The result was similar to a three-dimensional bar-chart although see-through and very complex.

Recall Cytoon offered, as the 'kiosk-wall' is formatted consistent with Soma-Location-IDs or SLIDs, many "kiosk-receptors" will be unpopulated at 'launch' time and Tag-Cluster populations at kiosk-receptors will be of varying intensities.

AIM then morphed the Kiosk-Harmonic display into a rectangular shape identical to the Kiosk-Pattern 'base-plate', except a transparent reddish-color, and then fit it to the Kiosk-Pattern base-plate.

One final rotation, of the newly formed "Kiosk-Assembly" showing our Emulation-Vehicle as blinking in the 'streak' representing our Tag-Cluster; then a spin around DiHol with chairs tracking to represent delivery to Soma-Response in-box and this segment of the journey was complete.

Definitely a great ride Mitoa said: I think AIMs scenario crafting helped make goings-on very clear.

> If additional information regarding the neural processes, which are active for both 'kiosk-receptor' loading, Kiosk-Harmonic and Kiosk-Pattern creation are of interest Vesi offered, link DD-006 is available on DiHol's reference segment, which you can access at your convenience.

Soma-Response: Level 3: Stage 2 > Task 2

I totally agree Mitoa Cytoon said; it will be very interesting to experience AIMs renderings of "Soma-Response" activities, as it has been doing amazing so far.

> No sooner stated than AIM presented and began rotating a cube-shaped object labeled 'in-box' on DiHol's upper-right quadrant, while playing the 'kiosk-wall' frequency scale. Maybe the programmers gave too much formatting freedom to AIM I suggested jokingly or more seriously I said perhaps AIM is actually being creative: a definite sign artificial intelligence is aware.

Interesting Cytoon remarked ponderingly. Anyway, important to remember before we continue she said, just as familiar music-note combinations or vibrational patterns are readily identifiable in totality, so does Soma-Response similarly accomplish Kiosk-Harmonic recognition: i.e., the 'harmonic' is accepted as a whole.

In other words, just as song recognition does not require discriminating then reconstructing each note of each instrument because one is immediately aware they have heard it before: neither is such rendering necessary for Soma-Response.

Resultantly, Cytoon continued the Kiosk-Harmonic is not only very frugal with neural-real-estate but also gives rapid comparative capability for complex information sets such as Bombardment combinations.

Vesi joined by saying incredibly Soma-Response and Sensory-Acceptance actually play similar vital roles. Whereas Sensory-Acceptance provided the interface between the 'Out-There' to the 'In-Here', Soma-Response provides the reverse interface; between the 'In-Here' to the 'Out-There'.

Soma-Response then she continued is the link, which by data-archiving or 'Bracketing' delivers the outbound part of the feedback-loop; whereas Sensory-Acceptance provisions the data-acquisition segment.

I expect the following four Soma-Response actions will be part of our next leg Cytoon said, namely: data-archiving, archive-updating and data-linking of Kiosk-Harmonics and Kiosk-Patterns; rapid location of the best-fit Kiosk-Pattern by employing the inbound Kiosk-Harmonic; and forwarding the Kiosk-Pattern suggestion to Soma-Response. Cytoon asked AIM to please continue.

AIM stopped rotating the 'in-box' and re-presented the Kiosk-Assembly. It detached the inbound Kiosk-Harmonic and sent it racing into the Kiosk-Harmonic data-repository to find either an exact match or closest-match.

Whether young or simply with minimum exposure to an external situation at any time during life Vesi said the Soma-Response search for exact-match will come up empty.

In actual fact Vesi continued, in that the complex is so very specific in terms of Soma-Location mixes, which configure the Kiosk-Harmonic, exact match is less than more likely except in situations where concentrated practice for years has Bracketed nearly every combination of SLIDS for the activity in question.

Even then things can go awry Cytoon said. Even though I am incredibly good at tennis and have played for decades every once in a while my shots just go awry because 'best-fit' is interrupted by some not perceived soma-feedback SLID injection, which creates a cluster of unknown exact-match Kiosk-Harmonics, which results in less than stellar pattern choice and thus Soma-Action breakdown contrary to my intention.

So if no exact-match, the only choice, as hinted at above, is best-fit I asked? Cytoon affirmed and continued by stating not only is that the case but Soma-Response is irrevocably mandated to send something to Soma-Action even if 'way-off' by 'best' standards. Additionally, Soma-Response doesn't get to ponder its options but locate best-fit and immediately send it to Soma-Actions in-box.

By way of corroborating our conversations, AIM displayed a small representation of a neural-array covering the upper-third of DiHol's sphere. Blinking shimmering red within its bounds was an archived Kiosk-Harmonic: AIMs rendition of displaying a 'best-fit' or not exact-match to the inbound Kiosk-Harmonic.

AIM quickly employed a replicant of the best-fit archived Kiosk-Harmonic as a beacon to pinpoint its linked archived Kiosk-Pattern: its similar neural-array representation covered the lower-third of DiHol's sphere. Archived within its discrete data-repository the located archived Kiosk-Pattern also blinked; but instead in vibrant yellow.

Shortly after on a small section of the center portion of DiHol AIM displayed an 'in-box' as before; except this was marked Soma-Action. With some fanfare, AIM pointedly replicated the best-fit archived Kiosk-Pattern, spiraled it around the open center section of DiHol and then dropped it in.

AIM was now in full stride as it accented both the Kiosk-Harmonic and the Kiosk-Pattern data-repositories by expanding their displays from one-third to one-half; except this time on the vertical plane instead: a nice touch I thought.

AIM then displayed the solid red inbound Kiosk-Harmonic as being added to the Kiosk-Harmonic data-repository by showing it snuggling in between two others of slightly different reds: AIMs way of showing the inbound Kiosk-Harmonic was being hierarchically inserted by frequency.

Similarly AIM presenter the inbound Kiosk-Pattern as being data-archived. Depiction of the link between the two was shown as a diaphanous thread, which I thought was brilliant.

AIM or the programmers or both outdid themselves with the rendition of Soma-Responses 'non-matched' actions said Cytoon.

Displays nicely showed the progression of events when the inbound Kiosk-Harmonic as a no-match: sourcing of the 'best-fit' archived Kiosk-Pattern companion by employing a replicant of the best-fit Kiosk-Harmonic; replication of the archived companion Kiosk-Pattern and its subsequent dispensing into Soma-Actions 'in-box'; and the archiving of both the inbound Kiosk-Harmonic and the inbound Kiosk-Pattern.

Vesi suggested the Soma-Responses 'matched' actions would be similar except the inbound Kiosk-Harmonic would access its companion archived Kiosk-Pattern and immediately deploy to Soma-Action.

Another aspect is evident though, Cytoon inserted, which definitely augments the benefits of practice. When the inbound Kiosk-Harmonic is a 'match' the companion inbound Kiosk-Patterns 'spire' action-potentials are accumulated into the existing archived Kiosk-Pattern, thereby yielding a more dynamic Kiosk-Pattern to Soma-Action on next access.

Definitely Vesi agreed, a 'larger' overall action-potential would result when 'spires' are accumulated, which would absolutely enhance Soma-Actions.

Excitingly, Vesi continued direct access plus 'larger' Kiosk-Pattern 'spire' action-potentials are the reasons extensive practice or experience directly instigate not only much faster but also more precise Soma-Responses; therefore much faster and more precise Soma-Actions.

Soma-Action: Level 3: Stage 2 > Task 3

Once again AIM presented and began rotating a cube-shaped object labeled 'in-box' on DiHol's upper-right quadrant, this time displaying a Soma-Action label. No doubt AIMs subtle way of coaxing us forward to our final 'recognized' and 'nominal-intensity' destination.

Soma-Action provides all interfaces to the entire array of possible soma or physical actions, Vesi offered. In other words, she continued every physical soma-location capable of being accessed by the nervous system is mapped and accounted for: ostensibly everywhere, in a healthy body.

Therefore, Vesi concluded Soma-Action is a "universe-facing" mechanism, versus "internal facing" mechanisms encountered post sensory apparatus.

Soma-Action, Cytoon expanded provides incredible and consistently precise implementation by exercising outward-facing "soma-connections". One develops from a zygote or fertilized single cell she continued by genetically determined cell division. As one develops so to do specialty structures, which form many interacting systems: sensory; nervous; endocrine; circulatory; respiration; muscle; skeletal; organ; etc.

All development has but one purpose I stated: survival within the bestowed hostile universe environment: or more specifically within one's ever changing 'Bombardment-Sphere'.

For survival one requires three incredibly honed stages I call the "interaction-cycle". It describes a path inbound from Bombardment acceptance I continued through neural-array processing; and then outbound to genetically linked physical structures designed for adjustment of one's interaction with the 'Out-There' in accordance with sensory-acceptance of Bombardment. It is a 'cycle-that-never-ends' while an organism survives.

More specifically Vesi contributed the 'interaction-cycle' begins inbound with sensory-reception, which resultantly fodders central brain-mass Matched-Base-Frequency neural-array processing; and continues, once Filtered-and-Slotted from brain-mass Matched-Base-Frequency neural-arrays, outbound to linked biological structures capable of adjusting appropriate interactions with the 'Out-There' as signaled by originating sensory-acceptance.

Cytoon elaborated by stating Matched-Base-Frequencies, which transition and coordinate data-flow are set in motion by both inbound and outbound mechanisms: Soma-Action is one outbound mechanism; Survival-Threat is another. Soma-Action then she elaborated resides at the pivotal juncture between evaluation and connection to the 'outbound functionality' of Matched-Base-Frequency neural-arrays.

> In other words, it is positioned between "sensory-IN" plus processing and "action-OUT".

As now understood Vesi kicked in a Kiosk-Pattern was generated by gathering a precisely 'time-sliced' array of Tag-Clusters, which represented a 'second-by-second' broader-scope of Soma-Location-IDs or SLID sensory-events.

Additionally, she said recall Tag-Cluster 'spires', arranged in fixed SLID-order by the 'kiosk-wall', carry action-potentials equal to sensory-event SLID intensity. Stated differently, it is the Kiosk-Pattern, which thus carries the Soma-Locations and their companion intensities for the specified range of bombardment-events, which will be used to correctly inspire outbound action.

As a Kiosk-Pattern establishes a direct tie to the original occurrence, Vesi said, it is brilliant how the Kiosk-Pattern is utilized to literally fit into Soma-Actions "outbound-grid" socket or "Action-Pattern". The 'Action-Pattern' configuration thus provisions a direct "plug-in" for a Kiosk-Pattern.

Additionally, Cytoon offered Action-Pattern structure is similar to the 'kiosk-wall': although order is identical; function is inversed. When a Kiosk-Pattern 'plugs-in' the intensity of each 'spire' is harvested, instead of accumulated, she stated to determine individual outbound action-potentials, which are then shunted to appropriate dendrites of genetically mapped Matched-Base-Frequencies.

In turn the allocated Matched-Base-Frequencies shoot the action-potentials to appropriate, also genetically mapped, Soma-Location "bio-groupings". Not only this Vesi added but action-potentials, when accepted by Matched-Base-Frequency dendrites, additionally and appropriately alert the

Endocrine-System: it is after all the power-house, which modulates action-potentials in accordance to SLID intensities aligned to sensory-acceptance and thus Bombardment.

> At this point DiHol came alive once again. AIM faded in and slowly rotated a new and large representation of the 'Kiosk-Pattern' in the upper-third of DiHol. It looked like the flat or non-curved business end of a porcupine or pin brush except, although the consistently spaced 'pin' sockets numbered in the many thousands, more than half the pins were randomly missing and those which existed were of variable length.

On the opposite upper-third of DiHol a minute later AIM presented a similar image: except no visible 'pins' and sockets were not only slightly larger than the 'pin' sockets but also color coded like the 'kiosk-wall'.

AIM then rotated each into parallel symmetrical position and slowly brought them together. As the 'pins' entered the awaiting sockets, socket brightness changed: longer pins caused a matching socket to glow much brighter than a shorter 'pin' when inserted into its socket.

> AIMs depiction was again eloquent: 'Pins' of course represented Tag-Clusters and lengths their intensity. Signifying greater action-potential, higher intensity triggered the companion 'socket' to glow brighter.

On the lower half of the DiHol sphere AIM rendered an image from the perspective of looking down on tens-of-thousands of dendrites with hundreds of neurons connected in the distance. AIM then proceeded to simultaneously discharge sockets into their comparable dendrite, which responded by flowing a representative sized sphere along its length through the axon and out the axon terminals.

AIM quickly repeated the scene over and over: 'brush' into 'socket'; 'socket's variably brightening; discharge; sphere traveling into and out of neuron. The light show was fantastic. We were actually experiencing Matched-Base-Frequency outbound communication. I wonder what Ernie was doing!

Journey-Two addendum:

Important to note, Cytoon said, at this juncture are the two possible channels for Tag-Clusters from Intensity-Assessment: either on to Soma-Slotting, which is Journey-One's directive or Threat-Check, which is Journey-Two's alternate divergence.

Recall, Intensity-Assessment was utilized when Recognition-Assessment employed Matched-Base-Frequency procedures (noted above) to determine 'recognized-status'. Specifically, Intensity-Assessment was engaged to evaluate whether intensity was above Matched-Base-Frequency 'normal'.

If so then 'amplified-status' requires additional evaluation by Threat-Check. Threat-Check will subsequently either assess a Tag-Cluster as high-intensity thereby thrusting it to Soma-Survival or 'Mid-intensity', which it will forward back to Soma-Slotting.

As Threat-Check will be fully discussed shortly in relation to the two 'types' of Tag-Clusters potentially arriving at its in-box, Cytoon elaborated, one from UN-recognized and/or high-intensity and one from Intensity-Assessment, we will wait until we arrive there on our next journey to talk more about Journey-Two implications.

Sojourn: SS-Three

I trust everyone Cytoon said enjoyed our sojourns through both the 'recognized' and 'low-intensity' and 'recognized' and 'amplified-intensity' channels. Even though, SS-One and SS-Two provided substantial insight, she continued much is still ahead. Tomorrow, after everyone debriefs and recuperates from today's adventures, the next quest will get underway.

Additionally, Cytoon elaborated, up to Recognition-Assessments evaluation of SS-One and SS-Two Tag-Cluster configurations, SS-Three activities are ostensibly the same. Therefore, SS-Three will be fast-forwarded to initialize from Inception-Filter. This time instead of being shunted to Soma-Slotting as a consequence of being 'recognized' with 'micro-intensity' though she continued the destination will be toward Threat-Check due to being 'unrecognized'.

Problematic

Good morning everyone Cytoon greeted as we were settling into our 'gyro-chairs': ready for the next journey? Please recall, Cytoon continued our ability to take the planned route to Threat-Check but not to "Survival-Threat" was made possible because science teams devised a methodology to reconfigure SS-Two orange-ester Bombardment as 'unrecognized'.

Ingeniously Cytoon said by way of appreciation, their solution was elegant by nature of its simplicity.

> Science team strategy was threefold: create a hybrid orange-ester molecule by eliminating one hydrogen atom from the original orange-ester molecular structure; configure the Emulation-Vehicles mimic-halos with the hybrids alternate vibrational characteristic; and create the desired mid-intensity Bombardment condition by simultaneously deploying the Emulation-Vehicles within a substantial amount of created hybrid mist.

As the contrived molecule does not occur naturally in nature, Vesi explained their theory proposed the hybrid Tag-Cluster containing the four Emulation-Vehicles would be 'unrecognized' by Recognition-Assessment and therefore shunted to Threat-Check.

Also, Vesi continued producing a large quantity of hybrid mist should result in greater than 'normal' sensory-acceptance and therefore a Tag-Cluster, which displays greater intensity or action-potential.

So, Cytoon said confidently, let's get under-way. Hopefully, she continued if the science-teams solution to present EV mimic-halos as 'unrecognized' works, 'problematic' will be assessed.

> Therefore, as soon as Recognition-Assessment evaluates our resident Tag-Cluster against the Matched-Base-Frequency data-repository we will know Cytoon concluded because if Matched-Base-Frequency determines 'problematic' we will be thrust toward Threat-Check.

Bracketing: Level 4: Stage 1 > Task 1

As soon as Cytoon reactivated AIM after her preface, chairs started gyrating in sync with a somewhat familiar display, which engulfed DiHol's display surface.

EVs within our Tag-Cluster 'globe' of identical mates were being hurtled once again along ever narrowing tubes within Soma-Cluster.

At each of the myriads of branching intersections AIM darted the 'globe' one way or the other as AIM presented its version of Recognition-Assessments quest to locate our Matched-Base-Frequency.

Quite suddenly AIM stopped chair motion and displayed our Tag-Cluster 'globe' on a pale red background within myriads of intertwined neurons. I believe Cytoon said AIM is indicating not only arrival at the correct Matched-Base-Frequency but also our specific data-configuration, although within its range of data-archiveable events, is not yet represented.

In other words, we are the first hybrid 'orange-ester' to arrive. This is great validation science teams' theories were correct, Cytoon commented.

Replication: Level 4: Stage 1 > Task 2

The 'globe' representing our Tag-Cluster was re-rendered by AIM utilizing about one-third of DiHol. The 'globe' was quickly stretched until it became two. The replicated portion was moved into an empty transparent compartment: AIMs way of representing the hybrid Tag-Clusters compatible data-archive; whereas the original was quickly dropped into a sphere, which AIM nicely labeled Threat-Check 'in-box'.

AIMs renderings are certainly easy to interpret Vesi said after commanding AIM to pause its presentation. Once arriving at the target Matched-Base-Frequency, AIM made obvious our Tag-Cluster was not part of its current data-resource detail by also dragging and dropping us into an empty transparent sphere.

Threat-Check: Level 4: Stage 1 > Task 3

Once again AIM provided just the right clarifying representation on DiHol. AIM characterized Threat-Checks 'in-box' by displaying it as a transparent 'sphere' with many differently colored and shaped 'globes', representing Tag-Clusters, suspended inside: however, far fewer than when gathered at Inception-Filter's inbound portal.

Additionally noticeable, the 'in-box' contained not only substantially larger 'globes' than did Inception-Filter but also their colors veritably sparked: like metallic paint on a bright sunny day.

DiHol's presentation clearly illustrates Threat-Check provides a place not only housing fewer but also many higher-intensity Tag-Clusters Cytoon said. She continued by advising one would hope fewer would be the case though as the preponderance of sensory-acceptance should be 'recognized' and 'nominal-intensity' during a 'normal' day.

Actually, Vesi stated, one should expect about eighty-five percent, give-or-take, of 'day-to-day' Bombardment to be 'recognized' and 'nominal-intensity'; thus handled directly by Soma-Slotting.

The remaining fifteen percent spawns from two sources, Vesi stated: Journey-Two's 'amplified-intensity'; and 'unrecognized' content determined by Recognition-Assessment. Both types will discretely arrive for evaluation at Threat-Checks 'in-box'. Hopefully, both the 'recognized' and 'unrecognized' portions will be free of critical 'MACRO-intensity': the topic of "Sojourn: SS-Four", she alerted.

Also very clear, Vesi continued, is we made it to Threat-Check: no doubt the science folks will be pleased.

Recall we arrived at Threat-Check, Cytoon said because either 'unrecognized' and/or 'extreme' intensity characteristics were ratified by Recognition-Assessment. Also she added, Threat-Check is a priority handling mechanism. Consequently, Soma-Self "Intensity-Check" and "Trend-Analysis" provide both enhanced processing speed and capabilities.

Definitely, Vesi interjected: variably 'higher-intensity' results when one undertakes new tasks or gets involved in some extreme activity:

otherwise the majority, about 85%, institutes Habitual auto-response or "Soma-Habit".

Intensity-Check

Actually, broad ranges of 'bombardment-sphere' interactions can become instigators of variably 'higher-intensity' Vesi said: such as, being given a new project at work; moving to a new home; climbing a new mountain face; taking a new route home; going to a new Zumba class; or being mugged.

Although 'unrecognized' does not necessarily carry sufficient intensity to engage survival-mode, except the mugging of course, she chuckled, 'unrecognized' will definitely produce relatively higher-intensity, which will therefore require additional threat evaluation to ensure appropriate mechanisms engage.

> Threat-Checks 'in-box' was definitely not a place for rest and relaxation. No sooner had AIM displayed our Tag-Clusters as arrived than 'globes' were vigorously thrust to the next stage.

AIM rendered our extraction on DiHol by showing 'globes' as travelling a short transparent tube with others ahead and many closely following. To accent quickness, AIM briskly rotated my gyro-chair once.

As my 'globe' quickly approached the front of the Intensity-Check line AIM rotated and displayed the approaching 'tube' section. It sharply arched upwards and flattened-out: something like a bobsled run.

> The flattened-out arching section however was littered with mid-sized holes, which I could only assume functioned as a 'selection-grid'.

AIM displayed most of the Tag-Cluster 'globes' ahead of ours as being siphoned into one of the openings: however, a few larger ones did not fit and therefore continued on past the perforations and into a 'tube', which reformed at the end of the arch.

> I assume the 'larger' Tag-Clusters are destined for Survival-Threat; whereas the remainder for Trend-Analysis?

Correct Cytoon said: Intensity-Check is the first of two Threat-Check intensity evaluators. Accordingly, Intensity-Check quickly Filters-and-Slots

MACRO-intensity Tag-Clusters to Survival-Threat first: and sends the "mid-intensity" balance to Trend-Analysis second.

> Not to worry Cytoon assured the Survival-Threat leg of the journey will be discussed when we engage the final sojourn after this trip is complete.

Trend-Analysis Vesi said is an extreme evaluator designed to reveal repeating or ongoing mid-intensity events, which as a consequence of "activity-duration" may also require Survival-Threat handling: If so validated, responsible Tag-Clusters will also be propelled to Survival-Threat.

Trend-Analysis

> AIM showed our now bright orange EVs as being propagated, along with many other 'globes', into a single conduit, which terminated at what AIM labelled the 'Trend-Analysis in-box'.

Trend-Analysis Cytoon specified is the process fulfilling the essential requirement to assess mid-intensity 'ongoing-occurrences' for danger. Even when an occurrence is not critically intense, she cautioned like a mild smell of smoke while reading a book at home, it could be, if continuous, the harbinger of disaster.

> However, for Soma-Self to accurately evaluate threat due to 'event-duration' Vesi stated requires a much larger range-of-comparatives than just processing Tag-Clusters individually.

Even when a repetitive 'event-series' is not critical, Trend-Analysis plays a vital role Vesi stated. It provides enhanced 'fodder', which alerts Cognitive-Self via Cognitive-Alert of 'problematic' conditions so Cognitive-Self can additionally evaluate the iterating Soma-Self sensory-events for continuity, transition, seriousness, enjoyment, etc.

> Thus Cytoon stated, vital to recognize for future sojourns is Threat-Check processors provide the link between Soma-Self and Cognitive-Self via Cognitive-Alerts from both Trend-Analysis and Survival-Threat.

Trend-Analysis is charged with exposing threats Vesi stated, which are simply not detectable from evaluating streaming Tag-Clusters individually. Clearly, she continued a survival threat may exist when Trend-Analysis is being continuously inundated with unrelenting Tag-Clusters from an array of same or similar Matched-Base-Frequencies even when only in mid-intensity range.

> I now get how a dripping faucet can suddenly become annoying: the unrelenting similar sensory-input provided to Trend-Analysis ultimately inspires it to produce a stream of Cognitive-Alerts of sufficient intensity to somehow trigger Cognitive-Self awareness.

I am thinking other situations, where one becomes 'aware' and wants to get away or make some kind of adjustment to improve conditions also initiate with Trend-Analysis: such as strong aromas, droning noises and even an uncomfortable chair.

> Additionally, I'm guessing ongoing events, which one cognitively finds pleasurable, also have their roots in Trend-Analysis Cognitive-Alerts: such as a good massage, a gourmet meal, a familiar tune, and so forth. None are survival critical but they do carry sufficient intensity to direct them to the 'problematic' conduit.

Nicely stated and very true Vesi said. It is exciting a process is available at the Soma-Self level, which allows for not only analysis of repetitive events but also passing collated assessments or "data-packets" to Cognitive-Alert: thus inspiring Cognitive-Self assistance.

> Although you did jump-the-gun to nicely slip awareness and Cognitive-Self into discussions, Vesi chuckled, full disclosure of Cognitive-Self functioning will have to wait until the next documentary.

To continue Vesi said, there is an 'however'. To successfully evaluate for trends without pausing the data-stream presents a conundrum or catch-22: Trend-Analysis must allow Tag-Clusters to both flow freely to Soma-Slotting and restrain them long enough to analyze for trends. A processing function called "Flow-Mirroring" provides the solution Vesi stated.

AIMs rendition of the Trend-Analysis 'in-box', although unique was somehow familiar. Covering the upper DiHol area, AIM placed a transparent rectangular cube with two sections. The smaller partitioned section positioned at one end sported four openings: one inbound and three outbound.

As my Tag-Cluster 'globe' entered inbound, AIM showed it being replicated twice: resulting in three identical data-packets. AIM depicted each being energetically launched into nicely labeled outbound conduits: one toward Cognitive-Alert; one toward Soma-Slotting; and one toward Trend-Analysis.

AIM could not have provided better proof of my postulate: I was sure non-MACRO intensity data-flow could remain uninterrupted, while still being analyzed for threatening trends Cytoon excitedly interjected.

As my 'globe' entered the Trend-Analysis partition, AIM made obvious its most interesting feature. Its end-wall was covered in thousands of regularly spaced small cubicles of different shapes and colors.

Augmenting this vista, AIM displayed thousands of Tag-Cluster 'globes' of various shapes and colors, some the same, floating within its 'reception' area. As AIM zoomed in on a small section of the "cubicle-wall" it was evident to me identical shape and color 'globes' were being quickly drawn into their shape and color compatible "cubicle-receptor".

Then at regular intervals the entire 'cubicles-wall' was launched out the back-end. In a very short timeframe I watched this 'Flow-Mirroring' cycle repeat many times: cubicles aggressively attracting matched Tag-Clusters from the 'in-box'; then a launch of the entire array out the back-end. Incredible was the scene when I looked at the "cubicles-room" because pending 'globes' were being pushed forward by continually arriving new Tag-Cluster 'globes'.

I quickly realized when AIM provided an expanded view of the 'cubicles-wall' back-end: 'cubicles' once again represented Soma-Location-IDs or SLIDs.

Not only this but the interval required to attract Tag-Clusters gave Trend-Analysis sufficient 'scope' to assess if repeatable events present in the MACRO range Vesi said.

> AIM presented an image on DiHol, which greatly assisted understanding of how assessment of MACRO-intensity could be accomplished. AIM displayed the flat 'cubicle-wall' as being launched: then shifted the angle to about thirty-degrees right and bottom-up. AIM then proceeded to display a "cubicles-platform" with each 'cubicles' action-potential, accumulated from 'cubicle' Tag-Clusters, as 'spires' of colored transparent lines of different thicknesses and lengths jutting-up from its base.

AIM then rotated the 'cubicles-platform' and fit it like a lid onto a shallow transparent open box with compatible openings on the side opposite to the 'lid'. Again by rotating, AIM clearly showed no 'spires' were long enough to poke through the holes in the boxes bottom. Interestingly, AIM panned in on the bottom-end and displayed it was also color-coded with variously sized splotches of gradual color shifts.

AIM quickly added another display to clearly indicate one additional evaluation. All action-potentials of 'spires' within color-splotch areas were rapidly amalgamated to form new 'spires' on a "splotch-platform" lid. This new but smaller 'lid' was then fitted onto a deeper transparent box much as was the 'cubicles-platform' above. AIM again clearly showed no 'spires' were long enough to poke through the bottom-end holes.

> The message delivered is clear, at least for this 'cubicle-wall': neither individual Tag-Clusters nor Tag-Cluster SLID groupings were sufficient to provide MACRO-intensity and therefore no need to alert Survival-Threat. Additionally, 'box height' was a great way of indicating the range-of-acceptability for Threat-Check purposes.

Well Cytoon said the AIM / DiHol combination certainly provides terrific enhancement to theories and support to many expectations.

> The last three sojourns have certainly shed much light on "How-We-Work", I said. It is incredible how genetics has designed and structured mechanisms, which are not only exacting and precise with their inbound data-management but also no less meticulous with consistent outbound-renderings, while maintaining both data-

integrity and speed. For-instance 'Sojourn: SS-Three' was accomplished end-to-end in less than a second: an astounding feat, I think.

I agree wholeheartedly, Retic. The consistent application of frequencies whether finely-sliced as for SLIDs or encompassing as for harmonics has provided me, said Mitoa, with a refreshed appreciation for this universe and its fundamental laws and drivers.

> I had no idea, Mitoa said, how tightly our neurophysiological selves so completely adhere to universe principals until now. You can be sure I will be sharing my renewed understanding to as many of my physicist associates as I can.

Vesi added the journeys have been amazing and enlightening. Up to these sojourns, I have mostly focused on the brain as the center of who we are and 'How-We-Work'. I now realize my focus was very narrow as the entire bodies neural systems are fully integrated by genetics to the brain and therefore are part of it.

> Incredible a sensory-event at one small sensory-neuron is kept discrete throughout processing yet can be associated with desperate SLIDs within a finite timeframe to ensure our outward interface actions are perfectly correlated to impact locations and originating intensity.

Your comments are hugely appreciated Cytoon said. One sojourn, number four, is remaining in this voyage set. It is planned to take us to and through 'Survival-Threat'. It should be most interesting and enlightening.

> I trust everyone enjoyed the 'unrecognized' and 'mid-intensity' Threat-Check sojourn, Cytoon said. Next up is Survival-Threat. After everyone debriefs from today's adventure, the next quest will get underway tomorrow.

Sojourn: SS-Four

Welcome back everyone Cytoon greeted as we were once again settling into our 'gyro-chairs'. Science teams worked hard to make this final journey possible she continued. Yesterday, Cytoon said, our ability to take the planned SS-Three route to Threat-Check but not to Survival-Threat was made possible because science teams devised a methodology to reconfigure orange-ester Bombardment as 'unrecognized' and not 'high-intensity'.

Today though, we want to get to Survival-Threat Cytoon said. Although preparation and testing was extensive science-teams once again devised an elegant solution. Apparently she continued, extremely high-intensity is necessary, much more than originally assumed, to propagate the UN-recognized Tag-Cluster containing the four Emulation-Vehicles through Threat-Check and onto the MACRO conduit toward Survival-Threat.

Their strategy required three stages: create a substantially pungent hybrid orange-ester molecule by eliminating two hydrogen atoms from the original orange-ester molecular structure; configure the Emulation-Vehicles mimic-halos with the radical-hybrids alternate vibrational characteristic; and create an extreme-intensity Bombardment event by simultaneously deploying the Emulation-Vehicles within a large, continuous and concentrated stream of radical-hybrid mist.

As the radical-hybrid molecule does not occur naturally in nature, Vesi explained the theory was it would be 'UN-recognized' by Recognition-Assessment and therefore shunted to Threat-Check.

To also have Threat-Checks Intensity-Check fire it to Survival-Threat rather than forward it to Trend-Analysis however required presenting a concentration of radical-hybrid mist to olfactory sensors over a thirty-second interval.

Vesi continued stating this strategy should induce greater than 'normal' sensory-acceptance and therefore Tag-Clusters, which display extreme intensity or action-potential.

To say Ernie was a little reluctant to volunteer this time after hearing the plan may be understating his position slightly Cytoon said. Although he did step up and volunteer once again regardless of reservations, Ernie did have a few pointed comments during and after his 'misting': she chuckled.

> "I thought my nose was going to burn right off my face" Ernie vigorously 'offered' to the deployment crew, while jumping up-and-down with eyes bulging.

It turns out 'pungent' did not adequately describe his sensation, I laughed.

One other item before we get underway Cytoon said still smiling: as a fair amount of SS-Fours journey is fairly much the same as SS-Threes, SS-Four will begin at Threat-Check.

Confidently Cytoon said, I am sure the science-teams solution to present Emulation-Vehicle mimic-halos as 'unrecognized' and 'MACRO-intensity' will work: so strap yourselves in tightly as I am sure AIM will have some interesting demonstrations for us.

Survival Conduit

Flight is normal in dangerous situations: run first; evaluate second.

Survival-Threat: Level 4: Stage 2 > Task 1

AIM presented Survival-Threat 'in-box' by displaying a transparent 'sphere' with only fifty or so differently colored and shaped Tag-Cluster 'globes' floating inside. However, although far fewer, 'globes' were shimmering and all huge by 'micro-intensity' standards.

Recall Cytoon stated Survival-Threat 'in-box' can receive from two Threat-Check providers: Intensity-Check and/or Trend-Analysis. Although Intensity-Check provides Tag-Clusters singly, Trend-Analysis can deliver in large bunches as well. In the 'singly' instance, Cytoon said, any individual 'spires', Tag-Clusters, exceeding 'cubicles-platform' acceptability-range will be shunted to Survival-Threat 'in-box'.

In the second 'bunches' instance, Vesi interjected, all Tag-Clusters within the splotch, which formed the 'spire', which exceeded the 'splotch-platform' acceptability-range will be shunted to Survival-Threat 'in-box'.

This makes great sense Vesi offered because it accommodates for Trend-Analysis being able to recognize not only the involvement of an entire SLID but also of surrounding SLIDs. Resultantly, larger impact areas, like an entire hand immersed in hot water, can be effectively recognized.

AIM made obvious this also was not a place for pondering. AIM immediately displayed Tag-Clusters being organized hierarchically by SLID frequency into a 'cubicles-wall' similar to that utilized in Trend-Analysis: except its cubicle-receptors and thus 'wall' were much larger.

The display on DiHol was incredible as it proceeded to rotate the cubical-wall into three-dimensional view and then 'launch' its contents as a whole.

Almost instantly AIM displayed the flowing transition of the cubicle-wall into two linked structures: a "Survival-Pattern" complete with its very long 'spires' and a "Survival-Harmonic", which was morphed from the Survival-Pattern.

No sooner were these created than AIM used another section of DiHol, as well as some creative gyro-chair movements, to indicate the inbound Survival-Harmonic was being utilized to access the "survival-repository" for similar matches.

> AIM displayed a scene to represent Survival-Harmonics data-archives, which looked-like the concave section of a large parabolic dish with hundreds of 'spheres' tightly packed on its inner surface. AIM then displayed three selected data-archived Survival-Harmonics candidates in blue.

AIM proceeded to quickly grab the Survival-Harmonics associated archived Survival-Patterns by displaying a grappler-like apparatus to access them. AIM then dramatically maneuvered the inbound Survival-Pattern to indicate its matching to the three possible data-archive Survival-Patterns: once located, AIM displayed the final Survival-Harmonic pick as green.

> Fascinating Cytoon said: clear is the created inbound Survival-Harmonic was used to locate three acceptably similar archived Survival-Harmonics, whose linked resident data-archive Survival-Patterns would be assessed for closest match.

Also notable from AIMs creative renderings Vesi contributed is the comparative process was rapid because the configuration framework of the cubicle-wall is standardized.

Also, Vesi elaborated, neither Survival-Harmonics nor Survival-Patterns had to be an exact match: as long as they were within the range-of-acceptability as determined by Survival-Threat. It would also be interesting she said to determine during future sojourns, whether this range fluctuates or is ridged.

> Once selection was effected, ours and all the other Tag-Cluster 'globes' forming the inbound Survival-Pattern were inserted into what AIM displayed as a transparent mixing-bowl where the selected archived Survival-Pattern replicant already awaited.

AIM depicted the replicated Survival-Pattern and ours as being quickly merged, hierarchically arranged and replicated. The original was precipitously thrust into Soma-Slotting's 'waiting-area'; whereas the replicant was injected into Cognitive-Alerts 'in-box'.

Incredible to see how this works Cytoon said. AIMs renderings on DiHol make clear the merged outbound Survival-Pattern not only intensifies the inbound Tag-Clusters by amalgamating the action-potentials of corresponding archived Tag-Clusters from the archived Survival-Pattern but also sends additional Tag-Clusters from the archived Survival-Pattern, which did not exist in the inbound Survival-Pattern.

> This means, Cytoon elaborated even at the Soma-Self level, experiences represented by an archived Survival-Pattern become amalgamated with a sensory-event as contained in the inbound Survival-Pattern: thereby yielding a much superior survival-imperative to Soma-Slotting.

Amalgamation also explains Vesi interjected why both knee-jerk reactions and overreactions to some unfamiliar event occur or why a similar event, which may not be harmful, can cause extraordinary out-of-proportion responses. She continued, when a sufficiently intense Bombardment-Event occurs with which one has minimal experience, like someone jumping out and saying 'boo', only a partial match to survival-repositories is made.

As the closest match will minimally represent the inbound Tag-Clusters but will contribute most of the 'spires' to the outbound Survival-Pattern, Vesi said it massively sways the contents of the outbound to Soma-Action Survival-Pattern.

In other words, in such a case the new inbound Tag-Clusters will only provide a small part of the new Survival-Pattern; whereas the archived match will form the largest majority. Resultantly, the way one responds will be completely inappropriate.

> I have a perfect real-life example, I said. All those wonderful people engaged in keeping us safe, the police, fire, military and numerous others, have participated in survival training. Even though these folks manage in what the uninitiated would consider extremely hazardous conditions, their Survival-Threat evaluator has not been miraculously suspended.

Instead, the effect of training, which is designed to present a broad base of realistic experience, creates copious Brackets in Survival-Threat data-repositories. Bracketing assists both their performance and survival-potential because when life threatening situations manifest the new Tag-Clusters will closely approximate the archived ones.

Thereby, when a new Survival-Pattern is created, it will be closely representative of Deluge instead of almost devoid of new information as would be spawned by unfamiliarity. Thereby, best-case Soma-Actions engage, which in turn will enable correct Bombardment-Sphere alignment and thus superior outcome.

This was a great example Cytoon said. It underlines although humans do not have significant Survival-Threat genetically provided Brackets or instincts, there is strong evidence some Eukaryotes do.

> For instance, the sea turtle: they neither have contact with their life givers nor do the parents provide any after-birth survival or life skill instruction. Yet, after being buried under sand for a few months on some remote shore, they fight out of their shell cocoon, crawl up what to them is a steep sandy embankment and make a mad dash for their lives to the sea , which they could neither know was there nor realize its purpose if they did.

These Soma-Actions were not learned or Bracketed through experience but instead genetically implanted.

Survival-Threat Archiving

Without any hesitation, once the selection was made, AIM showed the inbound Survival-Harmonic being nestled into its correct frequency sequence on the parabolic dish, which represented the Survival-Harmonic data-repository. Likewise, after replication, the inbound Survival-Pattern was data-archived with AIM showing the link between the two as a thin gossamer-like thread.

These actions also make clear Cytoon stated, are not only Survival-Harmonics and Survival-Patterns both retained in Survival-Threats neural-real-estate but also they work together to dramatically enhance the outbound offering.

Survival-Threat archiving makes perfect sense Vesi stated. Survival-Threat is the last ditch opportunity to provide information for survival.

As Survival-Threat is the last opportunity, Vesi comtinued, imperative is to remove all stops and send everything, which is both directly tied to the sensory-accepted events creating the extreme-intensity and anything else, which was important the last time something similar occurred.

Once again AIM spit us into the Soma-Slotting 'in-box'

Implications: Soma-Slotting and beyond

Noticeable immediately upon our arrival, Soma-Slotting's 'waiting-room' became very crowded and no longer 'peaceful' as it was when 'travelling' the 'nominal' voyage. When our outbound Survival-Pattern 'package' arrived at Soma-Slotting its Tag-Clusters were fired to the front due to Survival-Threat Tag-Clusters presenting extreme action-potential.

AIM displayed the Soma-Slotting 'kiosk-wall' once again: then dynamically showed all 'package' Tag-Clusters, as well as those pending from other sources, as being rapidly drawn from the crowded 'waiting-area' into kiosk-receptors.

AIM used another portion of DiHol to show the launch-side of the 'kiosk-wall'.

After launch AIM subtly rotated the resulting 'kiosk-pattern' to provide a three-dimensional view. Two remarkable features were immediately evident, which were quite different than other sojourns as were not only many of its 'spires' very long but also many more 'kiosk-receptor' positions occupied.

Notably said Vesi due to not only the higher density of SLIDs as provided by the many more occupied 'kiosk-receptors' but also the number of very long 'spires' presenting extreme intensity this 'kiosk-pattern' will instigate significantly different Soma-Action.

No doubt this explains Ernie's jumping up and down, and because the Cognitive-Alert will reflect extreme action-potential, his 'bulging' eyes.

It is incredible to see "How-We-Work" from inundating Bombardment through several mechanism manipulations to Soma-Actions, which were powered by sensory-acceptance, Cytoon added.

Endocrine-System

Recall Cytoon added unique "intensity-tailored" Kiosk-Patterns are created by Soma-Slotting as a consequence of the manipulations and outbound deliverables of three pivotal mechanisms: Intensity-Assessment, Threat-Check and Survival-Threat.

Stated differently Cytoon said these mechanisms provide unambiguous directives to enable Soma-Slotting, via Kiosk-Patterns, to instigate appropriate Soma-Actions, which are designed to avoid and/or cope with Bombardment-Sphere conditions from mild to hazardous-extreme in the case of Survival-Threat.

> Although "Neural-Systems" provide outbound directives, Vesi stated physical-systems are where the rubber-hits-the-road: i.e., they do the work of moving one to safety. Consequently, Vesi said outbound signaling no matter how comprehensive is not sufficient to deploy biological systems: they need first to be primed and then individually engaged in specific sequence.

In other words, Vesi said physical systems or "action-sites" are not designed to go from 'rest-and-recovery' state to 'maximum-output' without sustaining significant damage: however, they are designed to go from 'ready-state' to maximum-output with minimal or no damage.

> Soma-Self physical arsenals then require ramping-up or pre-preparation and then, once in ready-state, discretely neurologically signaled as to required participation from minor to extreme.

Also however the reverse is true Vesi said emphatically. Therefore, the Endocrine-System provides not only variable impetus to sustain action-site activity and/or alertness after neurological signals have ceased but also a tapering-off period so action-sites can 'gracefully' return to 'normal' state.

> Symbiotically Vesi continued a signaling system of a different nature, the Endocrine-System, provides the vehicle for both types of hormonal impetus.

As soon as Soma-Slotting fires a unique intensity-ranged Kiosk-Pattern outbound, it also immediately fires a "ranked-imperative" alert, proportionately intensity matched to its created 'kiosk-pattern', to the

Endocrine-System. The Endocrine-System, Vesi continued, then deploys an appropriate 'priming' hormonal concoction to prepare physical-systems for action. We sense this as an adrenaline-hit when first encountering a hazardous situation.

> As Kiosk-Patterns are enacted by Soma-Action, the Endocrine-System is again alerted to target both component and aggregate physical structures in accordance with SLID 'spike' intensities: thus ensuring smooth transitional motions.

As long as higher intensity events continue their influx, so too will Survival-Threat outbounds and endocrine signaling. Although both symbiotically serve to maintain a high alert state, both systems are subject to fatigue or "Soma-Stress".

> Greater numbers of both inbound and outbound neurons will exist in refresh-state; and muscle cells and therefore muscle systems will not only become hormonally less sensitive but also create by-products, which interfere with acceptable functioning.

Compounding the fatigue issue is Soma-Self's very limited neural-capacity. Resultantly, in ongoing extreme-intensity situations two conditions will cause information deficit, which both result in compromised actions: sensory-reception decline and inability to process inbound Tag-Clusters at any or all of the responsible mechanisms. Degraded performance will thereby result in decreasing, rather than enhancing survival-potential.

Transition to Cognitive-Alert

Additionally, Cytoon said because Cognitive-Alerts are also being issued for all but 'nominal' events, "Cognitive-Stress" may disrupt Deluge processing, thus negatively impacting survival-potential. Cognitive-Stress and "Cognitive-Survival" will be covered in the Cognitive-Self sojourns in the second book of this series.

The good news Cytoon interjected once universe adjustment is accomplished, by avoidance or positional manipulation to ones interface with the 'Out-There', 'recognized' will once again rule. Resulting 'normal' ranges will thus quickly return not only receptor and cerebral neurons but also hormonal states to 'nominal' range.

I thought it would be helpful Cytoon said for the team to provide a short recap of sojourn highlights as we ready for the next even more eventful and exciting Cognitive-Self sojourn series.

Recap with Transition to Cognitive-Self

Soma-Sensor varieties are many Vesi stated. They provide uniquely delineated zones of contact purposed to 'inform' what is going on 'Out-There'. Also she added, as 'Out-There' is considered to be pre-sensory events, internal-sensors are also included.

Our biology Cytoon said is laced with tiny Bombardment impact collectors or 'event-horizons' called SLIDs or Soma-Location-IDs: from which the abbreviated name is contrived.

Incredibly, Cytoon continued, each SLID receptor-neuron array is not only an ever diligent recipient of raw 'mechanical' Deluge impact-data when not in 'refresh-state' but also discretely identifiable by a unique frequency, which remains immutable throughout processing, data-archiving and recall.

Additionally, Cytoon elaborated, although common transmission conduits are utilized by all SLIDs (Soma-Location-IDs) to transfer sensory-receptor information to brain-mass, each ends at its own dedicated brain-mass, which only accepts its specific SLID frequency marker.

More specifically Vesi interjected Neuro-physiological sensory-receptor design provides SLIDs with their own exacting bent on a sensory occurrence.

In other words, Mitoa said, SLIDs possess their own specific and immutable frequency recognition signature, which forever identifies the acceptance location. 'Marking' thereby ensures identification of the specific sensory impact point, which is essential for both 'recognition' and recall. This strategy ensures a sound is not confused with touch, smell or taste: either during data-archiving or data-recall.

So when tasting something, cupping your hand behind your ear to determine what it is would not be so useful, I chuckled!

Exactly Cytoon chortled: however one additional critical measurement is also necessary; 'event-intensity'. It is highly variable she continued due to not only the types and quantity of SLID locations involved as a consequence of highly variable Bombardment but also the 'short-to-longer' term accepted event quantity, neuron firing patterns, on-duration and recovery time.

Even so, Vesi said event-intensity is not determined at time-of-impact but further up the processing chain in Recognition-Assessment brain-mass. Here, the quantity of neurons fired at each SLID within a few millisecond "time-snippet" as controlled by a "data-band" are evaluated to determine 'intensity' and therefore next disposition: to either 'nominal' or potentially 'problematic' conduit.

To summarize if I may I said, the Soma-Self cycle initiates after sensory-acceptance with Inception-Filter, which Filters-and-Slots all accepted sensory-data. Subsequently, I continued Recognition-Assessment directs the data-stream into one or the other of two channels: either to 'UN-recognized', which includes high-intensity or 'recognized', which does not.

Whereas 'UN-recognized' and/or high-intensity are immediately fired to Threat-Check as 'problematic', I stated the 'recognized' data-stream is shunted to Intensity-Assessment for additional evaluation. If its verdict is 'nominal-intensity', Tag-Clusters are shuttled to Soma-Slotting: those which are not 'nominal-intensity' are also sent to Threat-Check for 'problematic' analysis.

Great summary Cytoon said, however next steps are even more advanced. Soma-Self tethers to Cognitive-Self by creating two distinct Cognitive-Alert "data-package" outbounds: both shaped, although differently, by Threat-Check. Notwithstanding the content and imperative variances between the two data-packages, she continued both are designed to initiate Cognitive-Self assistance to "Figure-It-Out".

By issuance of Cognitive-Alerts, Soma-Self provides one-half of the

Force-of-Habit

which champions species sustainability

Cognitive-Alerts then Vesi emphatically stated, provide a valuable clue to purposefully and massively enhancing ones "living-situation" by underlining THE requisite to engage Cognitive-Self at will!

This theme, Vesi said, will be revisited many times in books two and three.

Detailed Discussions

DD-001: The-Senses

Each person exists inside their very own continually shifting "Bombardment-Sphere". Every millisecond Deluge presents chaos to our event-horizon, whose front-line sensors muster a series of incredible capabilities designed to handle immense quantities of impacts.

Force-of-Habits coverage ranges from sensory accepted bombardment as the fundamental building-blocks for all we are or have the potential to be through behavior, personality, thinking and sentience. As DD-001 provides a refreshing view of the true nature of our 'feeder' sensory apparatus, comprehending this section is strongly recommended.

Five 'senses' have been adopted by primary education as the "common-senses": Hearing, sight, smell, taste and touch.

However, there are substantially more. Listed alphabetically for convenience (with visual-sensors as well) these sensory workhorses are extensive.

Body sense or somatognosis; Cenesthesia or the general sense of existing or being aware; Color perception and/or differentiation; Cutaneous or skin (cold, heat, pain, pressure, touch); Equilibrium or awareness of vertical position and/or balance; Hunger; Joint or arthresthesia; Kinesthetic or muscle; Light or the capability to distinguish light brilliancy; Malaise or sickness sense; Movement or head or body motion; Muscle or muscular movement awareness; Pain; Position or posture, body position and/or attitude; Pressure; Temperature; Spatial or relative positional; Stereognostic or awareness of form and solidity; Temporal or awareness of relative time placement and conditions; Thirst; Vibration (pallesthesia) or sensitivity to vibration; Visceral or awareness of viscera sensations (fullness, etc.); and more.

Sensory-receptors are the critical transition-point providing event-horizons between the 'Out-There' and all mechanical and cognitive post sensory-acceptance expressions of individuality.

Without sensory-receptors there would not be any interaction with the 'Out-There' and therefore no experiences and consequently no cognition.

In the field of Neurology, the simplest and most widely accepted definition of 'sense' is stated as "the ability to perceive a stimulus".

Alternately, the more informative definition upgrades 'sense' to "any capacity, ability or faculty capable of perceiving some aspect of one's environment".

Unfortunately neither is supportable as iterations rely on a 'perceive' requirement, whose use regarding sensory functioning is simply outdated and inaccurate.

Regarding perceiving a single stimulus, neither likely a methodology will emerge enabling its scientific tracking nor will cognitive awareness of it ever occur.

In other words, Soma-Self sensory-receptors continually 'Filter-and-Slot' and collect much information (process bombardment) transparently (as do Cognitive-Sensors or visual-receptors), which simply never sufficiently intensifies to be 'perceived' by 'Cognitive-Self': such as, myriads of minor environmental changes, including 'normal' smells, slight temperature fluctuations, sensation of shoes on your feet or clothes on your body, etc.

To the Soma-Self "Inception-Filter" mechanism (discussed further along), these persist within 'normal' operating range or "range-of-acceptability" and therefore simply become part of sensory 'white-noise' (consequence explanations to come).

Discussions will detail how "normal-events" originating with "Soma-Sensors" are handled by Soma-Self "Habitual-Responders" (Book-One): whereas 'normal-events' originating with "Cognitive-Sensors" are handled by Cognitive-Self "Auto-Responders" (Book-Two).

Today with vastly superior and detailed understanding of our physiological (living system) nature than was available a hundred or so years ago, "Sensory-System" is more fitting term as it encompasses an entire "event-handling" chain.

Specifically, each Sensory-System uniquely employs aspects of the global "neural-facility" as well.

Additionally, other incredible features are provided: for instance, system-resiliency, which ensures long-term functioning for an extended interval (decades); self-maintenance; and transparency or silent background operation, which does not interfere with conscious processes.

Signals Don't Mix

Signals do not mush together. This is one of the fundamental physical Laws of Universe. Therefore, understanding signal nature is of critical importance.

> Incredible is corporeal core electrical functionality utilizes the same principles which have kept the non-corporeal universe humming for some fourteen billion plus earth years. It is the foundation of all we are.

The 'signals' term is utilized dually in **Force-of-Habit** to indicate action-potential is being either propagated and transmitted from sensory-neurons and/or from one mechanism to the next or retained in neural-real-estate "data-archives".

> Signals are sub-dividable into very close frequency juxtapositions without cross-interference because each signal has its unique carrier wave.

The most dramatic example is photons (visible light is part of its signal), which remain distinct even though similarly generated by millions of stars, because of this feature. In other words, even though the light from each star not only 'looks' about the same but also is similarly generated, each star is observable separately because over the trillions and trillions of miles the photon propagates its signals do not mix.

> 'Signals' are everywhere in our universe and actually differentiate everything one sees and 'knows': i.e., signals such as radio and microwave are known by most, which are coalesced and transmitted by current technology.

However, a vast array of signals delineating the nature of our universe is more elusive to the human sensory-system. One's very narrow (sensory) range-of-acceptability simply does not provide receptors for their detection: although they can be extrapolated.

> All possible 'signals' as a whole or more correctly all energy 'vibrational-frequencies', form the primary building-block of our universe without which nothing would exist.

The range of all possible frequencies is described by a linear-table concept called the Electromagnetic (frequency) Spectrum (light is the visible portion of the electromagnetic frequency gradient).

> Signals are building-blocks because their vibrational-frequencies do not shift around as energy gets coalesced into matter; but remain absolutely constant.

Resultantly, in inanimate and animate forms, iron is iron, carbon is carbon and oxygen is oxygen, and so forth. Even slightly variant ions of elements are readily identifiable to the standard for the atomic configuration (element) being examined. In other words we substantially still identify these slight variances (called isotopes) as the same element because their vibration is ostensibly identical.

> Incredibly, because energy is the building-block of matter, frequencies also remain rigidly constant at the atomic level.

This property is incredible because it ensures even extremely close frequencies do not mix but tenaciously retain their vibrational characteristics. Without this steadfast capability discrete elements, which form more complex compounds, would mush together rendering the combination undefinable.

> Not surprisingly the word 'element' means part-of-something

Instead, although their individual vibrational frequencies remain constant, compounds elemental vibrational harmonies are what become blended to form a specific "compound-vibration" constant, which forever defines and discloses the compound as unique.

The same Laws running the universe are also applicable to the way we function.

Therefore, the 'signal' transmitted from an accepting sensory-neuron is a unique harmonic: not created by the mixing of elements to form a compound but instead fashioned from the frequency properties of not only the receiving-neurons inherent electrical characteristics but also its surrounding intercellular fluid and non-neural cellular mass, which all provide unique contributing frequency properties (more in the SLID-patches section below).

Signal Characteristics

Critical to appreciate: the first task of a sensory-apparatus is to receive; therefore this function comprises only the initial stage of a Sensory-System.

> Importantly, each type of sensory-receptor is genetically created to acquire information within its specific inflexible range and condition set.

For instance, each Sensory-System front-end sensory-receptor deploys first as a transducer, changing its "range-specific" 'accepted' energy form (mechanical) to another (electrical) and second as a "signal-propagator". Consequently, only accepted data-elements are energy converted and neurally transmitted.

However, strict "rules-of-acceptance" are imposed: the bombarded neuron must be active; the bombarding data-element must be the correct frequency and/or classification; and the data-element must also provide sufficient energy.

Active

Sensory-receptor neurons need their rest too.

Although there are many receptors types accounting for a range from short to longer term sensations, none perform as perpetually open pass-throughs for stimuli.

In other words, all have variable activity cycles encompassing a receptor-phase, a signal (electrochemical) transmission-phase and a recovery-phase.

Keeping in mind their activity cycles are measured in milliseconds, which can be longer or shorter depending on sensory-receptor 'type', gives appreciation for cycle speed.

Significantly, if a particular sensory-location, say fingertip, only contained one sensory-neuron, definite and unacceptable information gaps would result, which would negatively impact survival potential. Fortuitously, genetics has provided many sensory-neurons in one's fingertip (and other locations) to accommodate the activity-cycle of individual neurons: i.e., while some are at rest many more are active and ready to receive.

Resultantly, acceptance of bombardment from many 'same' sensory-receptors creates a 'flow' of sensory-information or a "data-stream", which seems continuous.

Tolerable-Signal

Even when active, sensory-receptor neurons are picky: they only accept bombardment, which falls within their narrow range-of-acceptability.

"Tolerable-Signal" design therefore acts as an automated mechanical filter, limiting acceptance to only their locales specific competency: for instance, eyes don't hear and ears don't see; taste doesn't smell and smell doesn't taste.

Even with extensive sensory capabilities, one has receptors for only a tiny fraction of frequencies in the electromagnetic spectrum.

It is easy to hear a loud radio or truck passing closely but impossible to tune into the myriads of high frequency cell phone signals all around you: unless you have the specific decoding receiver.

This analogy generally parallels our sensory-receptors as well. The eyes, for instance, are without the 'decoder' to receive frequencies in the auditory range.

Genetically fashioned for each of our sensory-receptor types, the accept-or-ignore tolerable-signal attribute thereby also demarcates their specialty. Fortunately for us, this 'attribute' performs consistently during one's lifetime: through trillions of uncountable trillions of sensory bombardment-events.

This feature thereby ensures information from one type of sensory-receptor isn't generated to 'look-like' another.

Precise tuning range means the senses don't actually work together but gather bombardment-data autonomously. The illusion of cooperation is a tribute to the seamless rapidity of one's end-to-end filtering-and-slotting processors.

The mechanisms, which yield integration and meaning, actually engage much further down the line.

Threshold-Potential

Even when 'Tolerable-signal' is substantiated, a "sensory-event" may not be strong enough to 'fire' the neuron: i.e., present sufficient "Threshold-potential": like too light a touch to be felt or too low a noise to be heard.

Mechanical filtering of this sort is beneficial as it ensures sensory-receptors are more often in the "ready-state" for important survival events, not squandered by slews of mundane occurrences.

SLIDs

Ultimately, the purpose of sensory-receptors is to populate and transmit a data-steam to dedicated neural "processor-arenas" designed to receive, interpret, interrelate, evaluate and then do something with its determinations, which will enable one's seamless and safe movement within their Bombardment-Sphere.

It is therefore critical the transmitted information contain content permitting effective evaluation.

As bombardment 'struck' somewhere on the event-horizon, fundamental is for higher processors to be apprised of where: i.e., its impact location. If locations were not discretely defined, everything would seem like everything else: one big lump of noise.

Secondly, it is important to know the bombardment-event size: i.e., how big a deal it is.

In other words, was the event a short slightly raised 'noise' or a long very loud 'noise': i.e., its intensity and duration? Additionally, as hinted at above, how much of the event-horizon was affected: just the fingertip or the whole arm.

Finally, the data-stream needs to define what the impacting event was: a noise; a burn; a hit; etc.

Thus presents a substantial complication not sufficiently conveyed by the term sensory-input. Therefore, a new and more informative approach is herein offered, which not only encompasses all transmitted information characteristics but also persists to allow stability to "data-handling" explanations for Soma-Self as well as Cognitive-Self, right through to awareness and cognition.

Sensory-receptor neurons, although they initially perform independent acceptance, also form generic 'patches' (like a quilt), which are defined by their mutual ability to receive the same Tolerable-Signal and their proximity.

Literally thousands of 'patches' of various dimensions, each accommodating different Tolerable-signals, account for the entire Soma-Self event-horizon. For now please excuse visual-receptors as they are dealt with later in Cognitive-Self.

When pricked by a pin, no one has any doubt about the impact-location: one instantaneously (almost), no confusion, identifies the very small spot where the intrusion occurred. If the incident was intense enough, I understand in some rare cases a specific verbal response may be offered as well: such as, @#^*! Verbalizing occurrences will be discussed in Book-Three: "Force-of-Habit: Implications".

Therefore, as each 'location' is definable on the Soma-Self "sensory-grid", 'patches' will be renamed to "Soma-Location-Identifiers" or "SLIDs" for short.

So then, what are the defining acceptance and propagation characteristics of Tolerable-Signal for a "SLID"? Keep in mind, whatever these attributes are they must be unique to each Soma-Location-Identifier (SLID), otherwise signals would mush together.

Well known is upon acceptance bombarding mechanical energy is transformed to electrical energy, which initiates signal-propagation away from source and toward a "brain-mass" destination.

Notably, propagated signals present "frequency-signatures", which range as slightly through substantially different.

Discrete frequency-signatures for each Soma-Location-Identifier (SLID) are a consequence of not only the receiving-neurons inherent characteristics but also its surrounding fluid and non-neural cellular mass, which provides unique contributing electrical properties.

Additionally, receptors attenuate the base frequency in relation to accepted particle vibration: therefore, an apple of one type smells/tastes slightly different than another type; or an orange, different than a grapefruit. Thus impact location and impact type are transmitted by the inherent frequency generated by acceptance at each Soma-Location and thus become its Soma-Location-Identifier.

A signal flows in an energy soup provided by metabolism, joins with other same SLID frequencies (propagated by other receptor-neurons from the same SLID), arrives at the bio-habitual brain through a common nervous system with no signal overlap and is then directed down a frequency compatible channel to its genetically associated neural grid.

Resultantly, brain-mass processors are informed of impact location and type by frequency and thereby deliver content to appropriate frequency compatible genetically determined data-archive neural-mass. Information is thus successfully delivered by frequency/vibrational matching to processing and 'storage 'brain-cells', which store the exact same frequency-signature (more details to come).

Critical because when patterned responses are ordered-up they are the 'right-ones': and one does not scratch the end of their nose when pricked on the finger by a pin.

Propagating "How big a deal" is managed slightly differently. Understandably, no matter how small an accepted bombardment-event was, it is going to involve more than one of the many thousands of receptor-neurons encapsulated within a "Soma-location". As sensory-neurons activate either with constant output or not, no opportunity is available to determine the "impact-intensity" from one neuron.

> Fortuitously, if a significant event is underway one can be confident not only will greater quantities of sensory-neurons within a SLID activate but so too will other surrounding SLIDs be initiated. Resultantly, more simultaneously firing neurons within a same SLID as well as in additionally activated SLIDs will create more information.

Thereby, greater activity causes proportionately greater impulse flow, which is interpreted by higher processors as greater intensity. Duration is interpreted similarly except the data-stream will continue to provide information from the same general array of involved SLIDs: thereby also 'informing' of bombardment-event continuation.

Thus both originating bombardment location (SLID) and "event-intensity" characteristics are propagated seamlessly into the data-stream as a construct referred to as a "Tag", which strums a recognizable vibrational uniqueness. Tags then travel along ever enlarging nerve branches. As they individually enter the many expanding traffic trunk lines, similarly tagged signals combine or cascade their information into "Tag-Clusters" (more on this further on).

Ultimately, each back-end Sensory-System provisions specialized and dedicated neural-mass (genetically determined) utilized for processing and data-archiving or storage. Thus only macro 'transmission-lines' (central nervous-system) are commonly utilized.

This is additionally important due to a universe constant: greater signal intensity overrides lesser intensity. Humans are also predisposed by genetic and Neuro-physiological mandates to 'handle' higher intensities first. Thus this fundamental law-of-the-universe is critical to maximizing survival potential as it assures mechanisms will respond to highest-intensity occurrences first.

Below is a simple example of greater prevailing over lesser intensity.

Light a candle in a dark room.
The dark room was partially illuminated because
'candle-power' overrode the lesser energy of darkness.

On a bright sunny day light a candle outside.
Illumination will not occur because
the Suns energy overrode the lesser energy of the candle.

Thus both originating bombardment location (SLID) and "event-intensity" characteristics are propagated seamlessly into the data-stream as a construct referred to as a "Tag", which strums a recognizable vibrational uniqueness. Tags subsequently propagate along ever enlarging nerve branches. As they individually enter the many expanding traffic trunk lines, similarly tagged signals combine or cascade their information into "Tag-Clusters" (more on this further on).

Ultimately, each back-end Sensory-System provisions specialized and dedicated neural-mass (genetically determined) utilized for processing and data-archiving or storage. Thus only macro 'transmission-lines' (central nervous-system) are commonly utilized.

Sensory Action Timeframe

Notably, the real clue to grasping one's capabilities is by first understanding the "operating-parameters" of the entire Sensory-System.

As previously mentioned, one is being continuously barraged with energy and particles in one form or another: previously noted in the range of 200,000/second in a 'normal' awake activity state. So whatever system is handling this raging torrent will have to be fast: very fast.

A millisecond (one-thousand in a second) is short to us. It is hard to conceptualize such a miniscule blip when compared to our familiar minute-by-minute timeframe.

Although short to us, a millisecond can accommodate substantial amounts of bombardment because most electromagnetic frequencies (like visible light, cosmic radiation, microwaves, radio waves, etc.) tickle sensory event-horizons (sensory-receptors) at or near the speed-of-light.

> Most find speed-of-light (which is really a measurement of distance not speed) a little difficult to conceptualize because is not only its label ambiguous but also its constant so large. In a vacuum, speed-of-light is defined as the distance (186,282 miles or 299,792 kilometers) traversed by a photon in one Earth second.

The following 'spin' should make speed-of-light easy to understand. Picture yourself travelling very close to the Earth's surface at the equator.

> Travelling at the speed-of-light, you would be able to circumnavigate the Earth seven and a half times in one second.

This translates to travelling about 186 miles (982,000 feet) or 300 km (300,000 meters) in a millisecond. Interestingly, Earth dimensions, as well as time would mean very little at this 'speed'. Light-speed would be great when late...for anything but a dentist appointment!

By extrapolation it is easy to get an idea of how much 'energy-stuff' our senses must deal with in a millisecond. Considering energy is everywhere all the time means a 186 mile or 300 kilometer corridor of energy bombards our sensor-horizons each and every millisecond. Incredibly huge doesn't even begin to describe it.

To stave off overload and thereby keep us safe an event-horizon defensive strategy is critical: Protectively, receptor-neurons do not process all potential input (more on how this is accomplished later)

Although initializing acceptance transpires at the sensory event-horizon, outcomes only ensue after a long (but very fast) string of Soma-Self and/or Cognitive-Self filtering-and-slotting manipulations have been performed. Notably, in that there is an event chain at work, which has an elapsed time frame, we never get the news first hand.

Additionally more complex, Sensory-Systems can have multiple functions, such as visual-reception (discussed in Book-Two).

For instance, to encode their data-steam, Visual-Receptor multiple 'sight' types (four +) each accept their restricted portion of photon energy within the visible light range.

Additionally, once photon 'impact' is accepted and converted to action-potential, this 'signal' is manipulated by several layers of cognitive-processors and ultimately presented by another mechanism as a combined reality construct.

Without question, one accepts the construct as 'seeing' colors, black, white, brightness, shape, movement, etc.

DD-002: 'The Self-Duo' (large format)

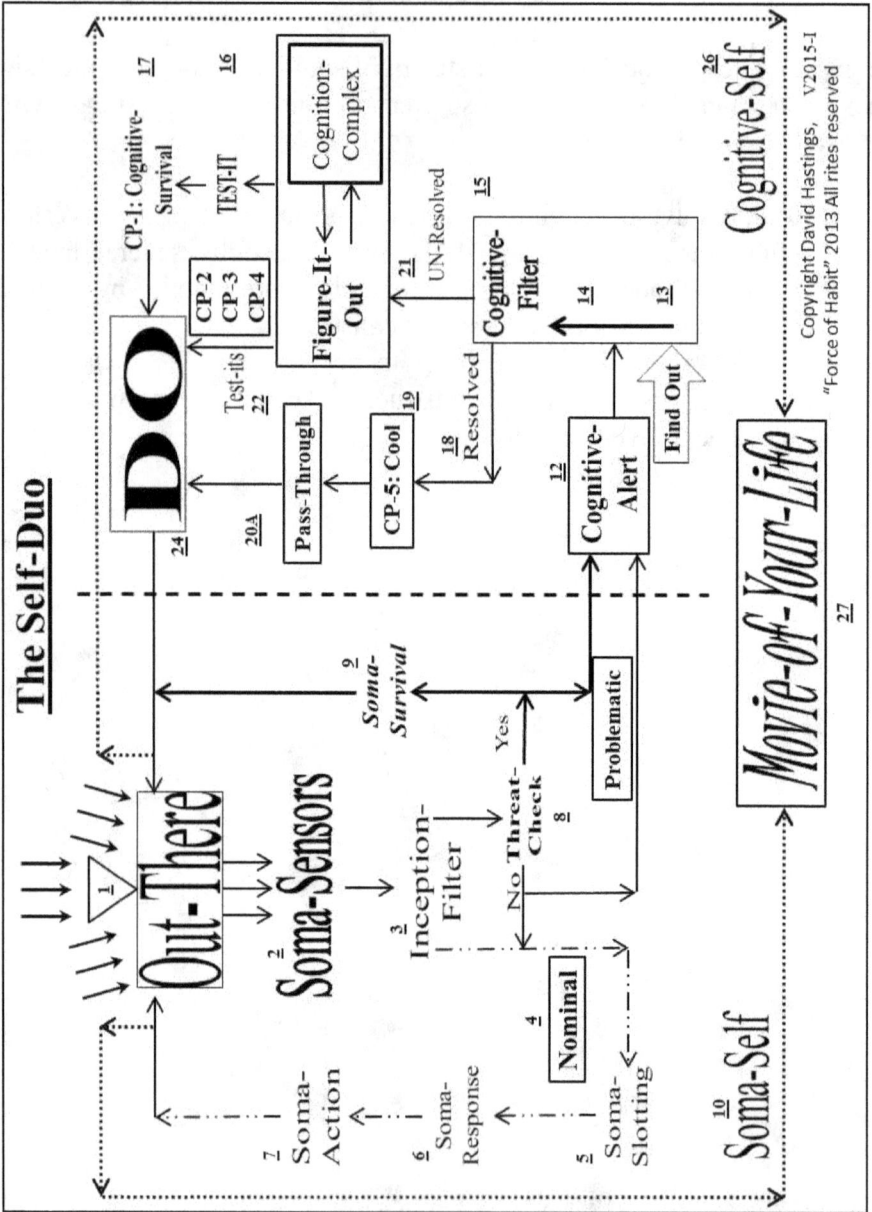

The Self-Duo

CP-1: Cognitive-Survival 17
TEST-IT 16
DO 24
CP-2 CP-3 CP-4
Test-Its 22
Figure-It-Out 21
UN-Resolved
Cognition-Complex
Cognitive-Filter 15
14
13
Find Out
Pass-Through 20A
CP-5: Cool 19
18 Resolved
Cognitive-Alert 12
Problematic

Cognitive-Self 26

Soma-Survival 9

Out-There 1
Soma-Sensors 2
Inception-Filter 3
No Threat-Check 8 Yes
Nominal 4

Soma-Action 7
Soma-Response 6
Soma-Slotting 5

Movie-of-Your-Life 27

Soma-Self 10

DD-003: SS: SD-LS: Soma-Self 'Self-Duo' Levels Summary

1. **Level 1: Stage 1 – OUT-THERE** (Self-Duo item 1)
   a. Task 1: Bombardment to 'Touchdown' on a sensory event-horizon
      i. Bombardment and consequently external and internal sensory-receptors require 24/7 diligence
2. **Level 2: Stage 1 – Soma-Sensors** (Self-Duo item 2)
   a. Task 1: Sensory-Acceptance
      i. Electro-physiological rules are strict! Only 100% compliance will enable acceptance.
   b. Task 2: Tags
      i. Where was the Landing Zone and how busy is it?
   c. Task 3: Wave-Bands
      i. Let's find out team and stick together.
   d. Task 4: Melding
      i. Hundreds of thousands of wildly differing sensory data-elements get sorted and grouped into Tag-Clusters
3. **Level 2: Stage 2 – Inception Filter** (Self-Duo item 3)
   a. Task 1: Ranking
      i. Who has the 'greatest-potential'?
   b. Task 2: Broadcasting
      i. Let's head out and find the rest of our team
   c. Task 3: Recognition-Assessment
      i. Seen this before?

No! Un-Recognized go to 'Problematic' channel
or
Yes! Recognized: continue, 'hook-up' and get intensity-assessed

4. **Level 3: Stage 1 – Recognized** (Self-Duo item 3)
   a. Task 1: Bracketing
      i. I know you: feel free to join your team-mates
   b. Task 2: Replication
   c. Task 3: Intensity-Assessment
      i. Just wondering if I am a little high-strung…

You are "intensity-amplified": go to 'Problematic' channel
or
You are only "micro-intensity": go to 'Nominal' channel

5. **Level 3: Stage 2 – Nominal channel** (Self-Duo item 4)
    a. Task 1: Soma-Slotting (Self-Duo item 5)
        i.   'time-slicing' shifts to second-by-second groupings
        ii. Kiosk-wall template
        iii. Kiosk-Receptor populating
        iv. Kiosk-Harmonic
        v.   Kiosk-Patterns
        vi. 'Launches' are consistently time-spaced and order-specific
    b. Task 2: Soma-Response (Self-Duo item 6)
        i.   Data-archiving
        ii. Best pattern location
        iii. Practice and experience win out
    c. Task 3: Soma-Action (Self-Duo item 7)
        i.   Plug-in seamlessly integrates
        ii. Soma-Slotting's Kiosk-Pattern provides the aligned data: Action-Pattern, the physical-world interface

6. **Level 4: Stage 1 – Problematic channel**
    a. Task 1: Bracketing
        i.   Don't know ya: let's find your place and get you situated
    b. Task 2: Replication
    c. Task 3: Threat-Check (Self-Duo item 8)
        i.   Does intensity signal a "survival-threat"?
            1. Intensity-Check
            2. Trend-Analysis
        ii. Cognitive-Alert sent

Neither test determines mid-intensity as survival-critical:
go to 'Nominal' channel

Trend-Analysis disclosed "MACRO-intensity":
dispatch to Survival-Critical channel

7. **Level 4: Stage 2 – Survival channel** (Self-Duo item 9)
   a. Task 1: Soma-Survival
      i. survival processes
      ii. Cognitive-Alert sent
      iii. Soma-Slotting

DD-004: Bracketing or what is this facility called 'memory'?

Firstly, I would like to clarify the following is not a comprehensive compendium regarding the intricacies of all aspects of brain-mass: it is however intended to provide clarification of 'How-We-Work' by explaining Bracketing and other integral processes.

Bracketing is the term used to indicate methodologies involved in populating or incrementing the action-potential of neural-real-estate data-archives. Bracketing either addendums a Tag-Cluster to its Matched-Base-Frequency array when 'recognized' or creates its first entry when 'unrecognized'.

Resultantly, if one was able to grab an entire Matched-Base-Frequency data-archive from Soma-Cluster, it would simply be called a "Bracket".

Therefore, as a Matched-Base-Frequency Bracket not only storehouses and preserves sensory accepted information, which was initiated at a specific Soma-Location-ID (SLID) but also references it for recognition and recall, a Bracket should not just be considered 'memory' but instead "frequency-memory".

Important to understand is a SLID and its Matched-Base-Frequency data-resource are intimately connected. Not by direct physical link, because an intervening transport-pathway (for instance the Central-Nervous Systems spinal cord) is between the two, utilized by all SLIDS; but instead by a much more elegant immutable backbone: foundational universe vibrational-frequency.

Digging into the structure of Matched-Base-Frequencies exposes they provision neither identical quantities of neurons nor equivalent integrating and supporting neural structures: i.e., some accommodate more neurons, some fewer; some extend outward significantly into other Matched-Base-Frequency territories, others not so much; etc.

The point is lots of variety exists. Regardless, Matched-Base-Frequency Tag-Cluster action-potential storage magnitude is not unlimited: i.e., a maximum upper-limit is in effect where repetition can no longer populate; but instead dissipate.

Compounding Matched-Base-Frequency variance, the fluid surrounding neural-cells often provides differing functional environments one Matched-Base-Frequency from another. In other words, different parts of the brain-mass are provided specific conditions, both chemical and hormonal, to frame their particular functioning.

> Think of the variances in Matched-Base-Frequency neural environments like fuel. Gasoline, which works well for its intended engine will not work well in a diesel engine; and vice versa. Another example: cooking oil is not useful for cleaning because its solvent properties are ineffective for the task.

Bracketing precision is phenomenal. One is genetically equipped with extraordinarily finely-tuned Bracketing capabilities. Surviving requires we be adept at identifying even the smallest nuance of difference within Bombardments massive turbulence.

> For instance, esters (scents) can be created in the laboratory. Synthetic scents are sold to manufacturers of products requiring the addition of smells to perfumes, foods, face creams, toothpaste, etc. Man-made esters however are not exact duplicates of nature's scents.

Even though an esters chemical formula may vary by only one hydrogen atom in twenty-two, difference is detectable to most: it nearly smells the same, but not quite.

> Recognition-Assessment competency is at the forefront of one's ability to cope.

From well before birth, early in the first trimester, Matched-Base-Frequency genetically dictated brain-mass connections are well underway. As organism growth continues, so too does nerve tissue.

Additionally, extensive SLID (Soma-Location-ID) to Matched-Base-Frequency brain-mass connections develop to potentiate detailed sensory/body/brain-mass communications and data resolution.

During pre-natal experience Matched-Base-Frequency creation and connection processes are very actively connecting and testing all the developing bits and pieces (pre-birth reflexive "kicking" is one example).

Bustle gradually declines after birth because exposure to non-familiar primary growth physical events also dramatically decreases. In other words, once were built development morphs from creation to expansion and maintenance.

Both Soma-Response and Cognitive-Self sentience require extensive 'Brackets'. Stored or data-archived comparatives are necessary in order to evaluate the ever changing (external and internal) environmental storm.

If initial recognition processing was not performed, our response interaction with the universe would be disastrously random and incongruous.

The ability to habitually recognize tiny variances is amazing. Smell recognition allows one example of the recall process. The identification of hundreds of food types and their various states (such as ripeness) seems instantaneous. One only needs to smell fruit before purchase to realize the effectiveness and usefulness of the Bracketing process beginning with sensory acuity.

A certain something is only UN-recognized once. It is an immutable fact the initial impression or impact intensity is directly linked to creation of a Matched-Base-Frequency addendums.

If the accepted portion of the bombardment was significantly intense, there is a much sharper 'memory' of the event, usually for years to come. Acuity is due to not only larger quantities of neurons necessary for storage of 'larger' action-potentials but also the establishment of much greater numbers of Axon Terminal/Dendrite (and other) pathways.

Many fears can be traced to a first shocking exposure to spiders, snakes, dark alleyways or such. These fears are hard to shake as potentially thousands of connection pathways and large action-potentials went into the formation of our first impression (Brackets).

Specifics

Although conceptually understandable, the above does not specifically tell how the energy-potential defining a Bracket is maintained at the cellular brain-mass level.

Data-archiving an inbound Tag-Cluster is fulfilled by accumulating its action-potential in as many available Matched-Base-Frequency neurons, those which still have remaining capacity, as needed.

Recall, a Matched-Base-Frequency is like a pool of neurons, whose fundamental configuration only recognizes a single exact frequency. SLID accepted signals (frequencies) simply cannot be received by any but the frequency matched Matched-Base-Frequency array.

> A radio transmission provides a useful analogy. A station transmits a predetermined specific frequency with enough power so it can be received (comparative: SLID sensory-neuron).

In other words, the expectation is one frequency (chosen station) will not overlap the signals (frequencies) of other broadcasting stations. If they did, sound-mush or useless static would be the result. Indeed it would be the same for us if a SLID and its dedicated Matched-Base-Frequency receiver were not in perfect frequency alignment but instead received randomly.

DD-005: Sensory-Interaction Complexity 'Short-List'

> Bombardment produces copious, ongoing, multi-active and potentially multiplexed sensory-events.

In other words, huge quantities of SLIDs are continually active, which may or may not be providing correlated data-flow. Additionally, sensory-events capture a wide Deluge activity range from fewer while asleep to overwhelming as when bungee jumping for the first time.

Explanations of the Neuro-Physiological mechanism operations (et al) responsible for providing millisecond evaluations and responses, which accommodate this incredibly broad-scope is needed: a selection of sensory-event fluctuations and complexities follows.

Bombardment-Sphere Deluge can:
- instantaneously range from minimal, total silence and darkness to maximum, extreme noise and brightest light
- be of short to long duration: for instance, a car horn toot to an Tsunami warning siren
- range from nearly imperceptible to intense: touching a feather with a fingertip to shutting a car door on a finger
- be compounded: hearing your name called while in a noisy crowd
- initialize all senses simultaneously: Some sensory-data may be co-ordinated yet remain discrete: i.e., operative for fewer or multiple events. For instance, one can be listening to favorite music, while looking at the sunset, while smelling a scented candle, while enjoying the taste of wine, while realizing new shorts are too tight because of eating too much, all while enjoying the company of a significant other

Additionally, how does an event suddenly intensify or de-intensify; how can event changes be experienced, remembered and evaluated over time; how do we become more aware of danger as events unfold; how is such complexity sorted out; how is management even possible; etc.?

Each book in the **Force-of-Habit** series will present explanations from various perspectives to explain these as well as many other continuous and variable interactions with one's Bombardment-Sphere.

DD-006: Biological System Performance is Oxygen Critical

Just as flint is the impetus causing a spark by the interaction of oxygen when struck against iron, oxygen is the spark of metabolic life. Metabolic processes require this 'heavy' atom to be readily available: otherwise life ceases within minutes.

> Although most consider us a carbon based species, I challenge this determination. In actual fact from the point of view of 'mass' (weight) we are an oxygen based species.

This is directly supportable from many perspectives. First, one's biological container by mass is about 65% oxygen and only about 18% carbon. Secondly, the body is comprised of 75% water give or take under normal conditions, which is also essential for life. Interestingly, the water molecule is about 89 percent oxygen by mass and therefore only 11% hydrogen: with no carbon to be found. Thirdly, nearly all (99.9%) of all metabolic processes require oxygen as the reaction spark: not carbon.

> Succinctly stated then, oxygen is THE primary life sustainer.

Its abundance maintains health...
its lack produces illness

Accepting all this then...so what? Fair question: Point is discussing How-We-Work from Soma-Self and Cognitive-Self perspectives would be moot if How-We-Work biologically was neglected. If one can enhance their biological systems it stands to reason Cognitive-Systems will also comparatively enhance.

> As Oxygen is 65% of body weight and used for most metabolism; and as water makes up about 75% of one's body weight, these aspects are obviously the two largest contributors to either health or illness.

Clean water is obvious as few seek out drinking murky questionable water. However, what about oxygen?

At first glance it seems we get enough...but do we....or are we just barely getting by? Are our metabolic systems struggling for years with insufficient oxygen resources thus ultimately succumbing to illness and early death in one's sixties, seventies or eighties?

Science has proven this natural substance called oxygen can be breathed in at 100% concentration all day long: not only without any negative side effects but contrarily with hugely beneficial results.

> These include rapid healing, better vision, heightened senses and vastly improved metabolism, immune system, digestion, circulation, muscle strength and so on and so on.

Interestingly though 'all day long' is not necessary for optimal health. Instead about 9 hours per month in 6 one-and-one-half hour increments while snoozing or watching T.V in a "Proper Hyperbaric Oxygenation" chamber seems optimal. This is because residual positive effects of short term oxygen saturation sustain.

> Don't be fooled though: there are many imposters. "Proper Hyperbaric Oxygenation" means being enclosed in a hyperbaric chamber, especially designed to withstand at least two-point-five atmospheres of pressure while being immersed in a 100% oxygen environment for about one and a half hours. Anything less is simply not 'proper' or maximally beneficial: and therefore not worth the cost

Why not just breathe more deeply for a period of time?

It would be great if that worked but it doesn't for quite a number of reasons. The first clue is obtained by explaining why 'Proper Hyperbaric Oxygenation' works every time.

The 'worker-bees' so to speak, which attract the oxygen through lung membranes (red blood cells) and traverse it around the body through the 60,000 miles (100,000 kilometers) of tubes (circulatory system) 3 times a minute fairly much work at peak capacity 24/7.

Therefore, breathing more deeply only arrests the two arterial chemoreceptors responsible for monitoring carbon-dioxide levels and responsively enacting the breathing function: therefore such attempts have minimal effect on increasing circulatory oxygen levels.

Additionally, we live on almost the lowest survivable concentration of oxygen in the air we breathe: about 20%. Remember our metabolism will happily uptake and utilize 100% concentration for extended periods and use it to optimize internal functioning and almost immediately make us healthier.

Actually, our amazing oxygen uptake system is continually stressed, trying to maximize the available weak oxygen conditions.

All one has to do is go for a short hike up a mountain (3000 feet or 900 meters) to experience tougher breathing conditions: breathable atmosphere is unfortunately incredibly thin! Couple this with massive pollution and, well, you get the picture: body stress as a consequence of the decline in a basic oxygen necessity is enormous!

Tissues are struggling to 'breathe' in poor oxygen environments, which is anything below about 50%: as our air is only 20% they are continually in duress

Fortunately, an easy solution is available: "Proper Hyperbaric Oxygenation". It works because it does not rely on red blood cells to carry life-giving oxygen but instead infuses oxygen into the fluid (called plasma) carrying the 'worker-bees'.

This is effective because where red blood cells must squish themselves into and through small channels (capillaries), free oxygen in the plasma does not. To help visualize the difference let's do a relative size comparison between the two.

If we determine the free oxygen atom to be the size of a regular stick pen, then the red blood cell would equate to a forty story skyscraper.

Therefore, regardless of capillary restriction or damage, free oxygen will get to the suffocating tissues where the cells will uptake the free oxygen and expedite repair as needed.

There is no magic to this strategy: if copious amounts of oxygen can be delivered to the starving tissues; exponential repair will proceed: if not, tissues will die.

The only effective and totally safe in every way methodology to accomplish this delivery is...you guessed it..."Proper Hyperbaric Oxygenation".

Do it for life!

Index

Index

Notes:

Notes:

www.ingramcontent.com/pod-product-compliance
Lightning Source LLC
Chambersburg PA
CBHW060859280326
41934CB00007B/1116